American PASSENGER TRAIN EQUIPMENT

1940s-1980s

PATRICK C. DORIN

Iconografix

Iconografix
PO Box 446
Hudson, Wisconsin 54016 USA

Library of Congress Control Number: 2010930575

ISBN-13: 978-1-58388-263-4
ISBN-10: 1-58388-263-4

10 11 12 13 14 15 6 5 4 3 2 1

Printed in China

On the cover:

C-1: The Northern Pacific's observation lounge sleeping car #390 for the North Coast Limited.
C-2: Duluth, Missabe & Iron Range Railway coach #33.
C-3: Spokane, Portland and Seattle Railway baggage-express car #60.
C-4: Algoma Central coach, a former Canadian Pacific coach.
C-5: Nickel Plate Road streamlined Pullman sleeping car. *Frank Schnick*
C-6: Great Northern Railway business car #A-10.
C-7: Great Northern Railway 60-seat coach #1115.
C-8: Alaska Railroad dining car.
C-9: Chicago and North Western parlor car #6700.

TABLE OF CONTENTS

DEDICATION

Dedicated to Toby and Sharon Marcovich, long-time friends.

ACKNOWLEDGEMENTS

Several people provided information and photos for use in this book. Without their kind assistance the book would not have been possible. The author wishes to thank each and everyone for their time, wisdom and the use of many photos.

Bill Jelinek, William Raia, Harold K. Vollrath, William Kuba, W. C. Whittaker, Anna Whittaker, Jim Scribbins, Jeffrey M. Koeller, Michele Pearson of the Lake Superior Railroad Museum, Dan Mackey, John Sward, David Bruns, Frank Schnick, Dale Wilson, Cliff Black of Amtrak and John Parsons of the Northern Indiana Commuter Transportation District. Should any name have been missed, the author apologizes and trusts it will be found at the appropriate location within the book. Again thank you.

INTRODUCTION

The purpose of this book is to illustrate with photos, drawings and other information for the different types of passenger cars in operations from the 1940s and into the 1980s, when this type of equipment began operating on Amtrak trains. The book also takes a look at some of the Alaska Railroad passenger equipment, some of which was purchased from other railroads; and new passenger cars with the same type of interior and exterior designs and size. The illustrations include information such as dimensions, passenger seating capacities, heating and air-conditioning systems, and the types of train services. Each chapter explores the various types of equipment in each category.

Beginning in the late 1930s, the new streamlined, lightweight passenger equipment was in the process of being designed and moving forward for production by a number of companies. These included Pullman Standard, American Car and Foundry and the Budd Company, to name a few that were in operation in North America. The steel cars had been in production since before the 1920s, and were the base design for new passenger equipment into the mid-1930s, when the first streamlined cars began to be placed in operation. In fact, some of the first streamliners that went into operation by the late 1930s included trains such as the Milwaukee Road Hiawathas and the Burlington Route Zephyrs.

World War II sidetracked a great deal of the potential passenger car orders, but once the war was over; new streamlined passenger equipment was rolling off the assembly lines. New streamliners went into service throughout all of North America.

Trains, such as the Great Northern's Empire Builder, once equipped with heavyweight cars, became a new generation of streamliners.

The new streamlined cars soon became mixed with the heavyweight cars. Many passenger trains operated with such mixtures. There are many examples of train consists of overnight trains, secondary transcontinental, corridor trains, commuter trains and more.

The interiors of the many passenger cars included all types of coach seating, including leg-rest seats for overnight and transcontinental trains. Dining and lounge cars were configured as either full dining cars or lounge cars, but were also designed as combination diner-lounges, sometimes designated as café lounge cars. Food service cars included a variety of interiors with different titles, such as coffee-shop cars, and restaurant-lounge cars. In fact, food and beverage facilities were often part of a combination design, such as a sleeper lounge observation, sleeper restaurant lounge, or a parlor observation lounge car. This is only a partial list of the types of combinations of accommodations.

Other types of combination cars included coach-baggage cars, and baggage dormitory cars. The latter included sleeping accommodations for the long distance train crews. There were even combination doach-sleeping cars, which operated on overnight trains with relatively low numbers of passengers. One example was the Duluth, South Shore and Atlantic Railway's overnight Duluth, Minnesota-Marquette, Michigan train known as the North Country Mail.

Finally, there is much to learn from the passenger car designs of the years gone by. They were very comfortable cars and smooth running. In fact, much of the streamlined passenger equipment was capable of operating at speeds of up to 120 miles per hour or higher. Many folks have the impression that high-speed trains were invented by Japan and France. With the appropriate signal systems, and well-built track, trains speeds could be as high as 110 to 120 miles per hour. This was once common on routes such as the Pennsylvania Railroad, Santa Fe, the Burlington Route and the Milwaukee Road.

The designs from the 1930s and on into the 1950s could also be used for ideas for new equipment in the 21st Century. Just one example of the use of basic designs are some the Alaska Railroad Coaches built in 1989-90 (See Chapter 11).

The combination of the various types of equipment can also provide model railroaders with some new ideas of how to create passenger trains. The mixture of streamlined and standard heavyweight cars provided some rather interesting consists on many types of passenger trains, including commuter operations, overnights, day time, and transcontinental trains.

Happy Railroading,
Patrick C. Dorin
Superior, Wisconsin
December, 2009

Chapter 1
BAGGAGE, MAIL and EXPRESS CARS

Passenger trains not only carried passengers, but also provided baggage service for the passengers and space for express shipments and the U.S. mail. The equipment designed for this service is known as "head-end" cars since most of the time, the cars were placed at the head of the train. Depending upon the time of day, needs, and service levels, the number of head-end cars could vary from one to as many as ten (or even more) coupled to the motive power.

The baggage cars were operated for passenger luggage and railway express shipments. Nearly all passenger trains included at least one baggage car, with the exception of commuter trains. However, there were many cases where certain commuter trains also had a baggage car as part of the consist for delivering newspapers, and even express shipments, to some of the suburbs.

The U.S. mail and Canadian mail was handled in two types of cars. The primary mail car was the "railway post office." The RPO (as they were called) was staffed by a mail crew who sorted the mail while the train was en route. Mail was loaded at the origin prior to departure. The crew sorted the mail for the individual station stops, placed it into mail bags and dropped them off at the appropriate destination. At the same time, mail was picked up at each station and would be sorted for the various destinations.

When a train did not have a scheduled stop at a particular station, but mail was to be delivered and picked-up, the procedure was to drop off the mail on the station platform and pick up the outbound mail bag on a rack next to the track. The RPO cars had a flexible arm at the doorway that could reach out and connect with the mail bag without stopping. The bag would be taken into the car, and the mail would be sorted out.

The mail traffic was an important part of the passenger train business right through to the late 1960s, when the Postal Service began eliminating the RPO operations for the use of trucks for transit and hub centers for sorting. In many cases, this is less economical energy-wise depending upon the route of the mail for sorting. For example, a letter mailed from Ashland, Wisconsin to Superior, Wisconsin (a distance of 65 miles) travels from Ashland to Eau Claire for sorting, and then to Superior. The total round trip distance is 300 miles—150 miles each way.

The second system for handling mail was the use of "mail storage" transport. In this case, the pre-sorted mail from the Post Office was loaded into either baggage cars or box express cars. The cars were secured and were unloaded at the destination. Storage mail is still part of the railroad business in the 2000s through the use of trucks or containers on flat cars. It is no longer handled by Amtrak, which once handled the mail with Road Railer —trailers riding on rail bogies on track.

RPO cars could either be a combination of RPO and a baggage section, or a full RPO car. The combination cars had RPO sections of either15 or 30 feet, plus 55 feet or 40 feet of baggage space for a common 75-foot long car. There were some streamlined RPO baggage cars with a 60-foot RPO section with about 20 feet of space for baggage, express or even storage mail in the 85-foot configuration. There were also streamlined cars in the 75- to 85-foot categories with either a 15-foot or a 30-foot RPO section.

There were also 60-foot full RPO cars without any baggage space. These were basically 60-foot cars with the entire car devoted to mail sorting. There were both streamlined and standard heavyweight cars with this type of configuration.

Standard heavyweight baggage cars came in 60- to 80-foot lengths. Generally there were two doors on each side, but sometimes three depending upon the design.

Streamlined baggage cars were built in the 75- to 85-foot lengths.

Box express cars were basically freight cars rebuilt with high-speed passenger car or freight car trucks, and equipped with steam lines for operating on the head-end of passenger trains. The cars were normally in the 40- or 50-foot range. The cars were operated for both express and storage mail.

Trains devoted to mail and express, and often known as the "fast mail," operated with anywhere from 10 to 30 head-end cars with 1 to 4 RPO cars depending upon the service needs. Generally the trains operated with one or two coaches, but there were some mail trains without coach services.

There were some mail and express trains that were relatively short. One example was the Northern Pacific's overnight train between Duluth and Minneapolis-St. Paul. The consist included two or three baggage cars, one RPO-baggage and one or two coaches. A through Duluth-Chicago baggage car, loaded with mail, operated over the Milwaukee Road between St. Paul and Chicago. Thus one could observe the Morning Hiawatha departing St. Paul for Chicago with a NP baggage car as part of the head-end consist.

Mail trains often had a substantial mix of equipment from other rail lines for through service. For example, the Great Northern's fast mail could be observed with New York Central, Erie-Lackawanna, Pennsylvania, and other eastern and southern lines with mail destined for the west coast.

As a final note, head-end cars could sometimes be observed on the rear of passenger trains. This usually meant that the cars would be switched out or were picked up at various stations along the route. This type of operation saved time without having to have a car loaded or unloaded at various stops. The cars were on the rear-end because it was easier to back into siding for setting out, or picking up at the station.

The following photos and diagrams illustrate the various types of head-end cars in operation throughout the 1940s and into the Amtrak era.

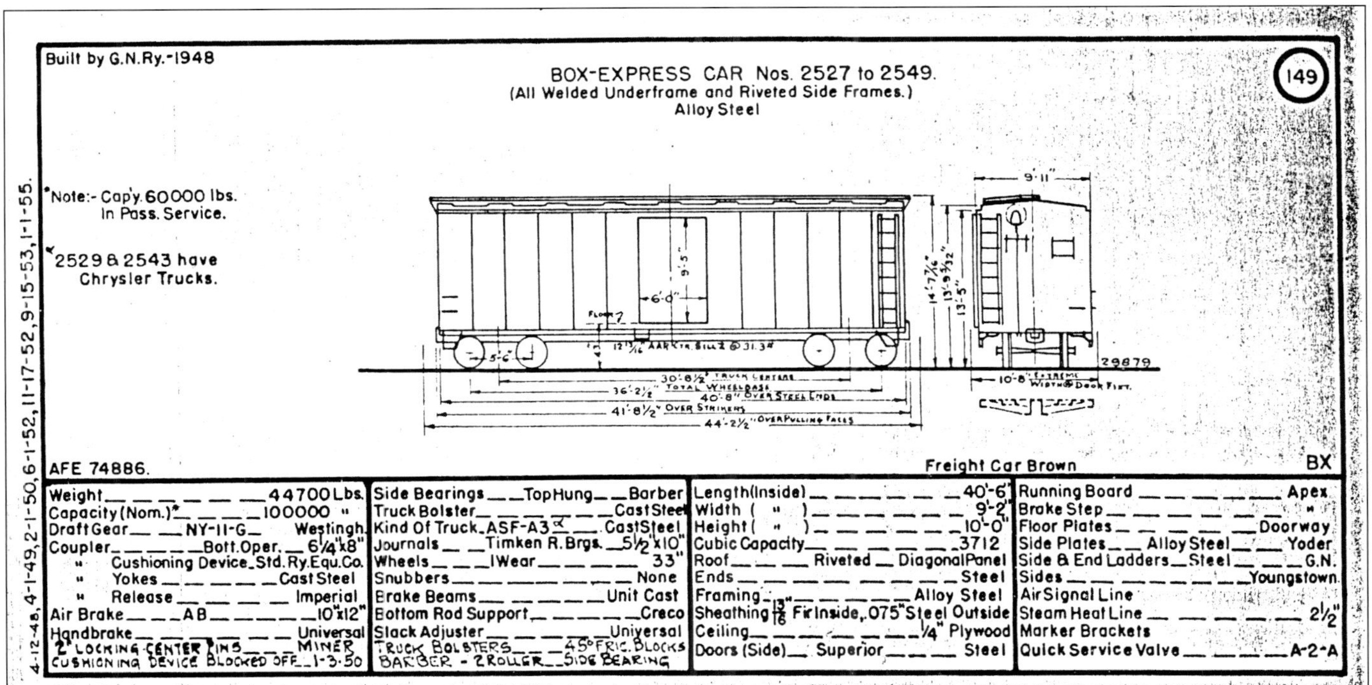

Forty- and fifty-foot box cars were often converted for express and mail storage service and painted in the passenger equipment colors. This diagram illustrates a 40-foot car with 6-foot doors. The cars were equipped with high-speed trucks (wheel assemblies) and with steam lines. With the steam lines, the cars could be operated on the head-end of passenger trains as the steam from either steam locomotives or diesels could be sent back to the passenger cars for heating. *Great Northern Diagram, Author's Collection*

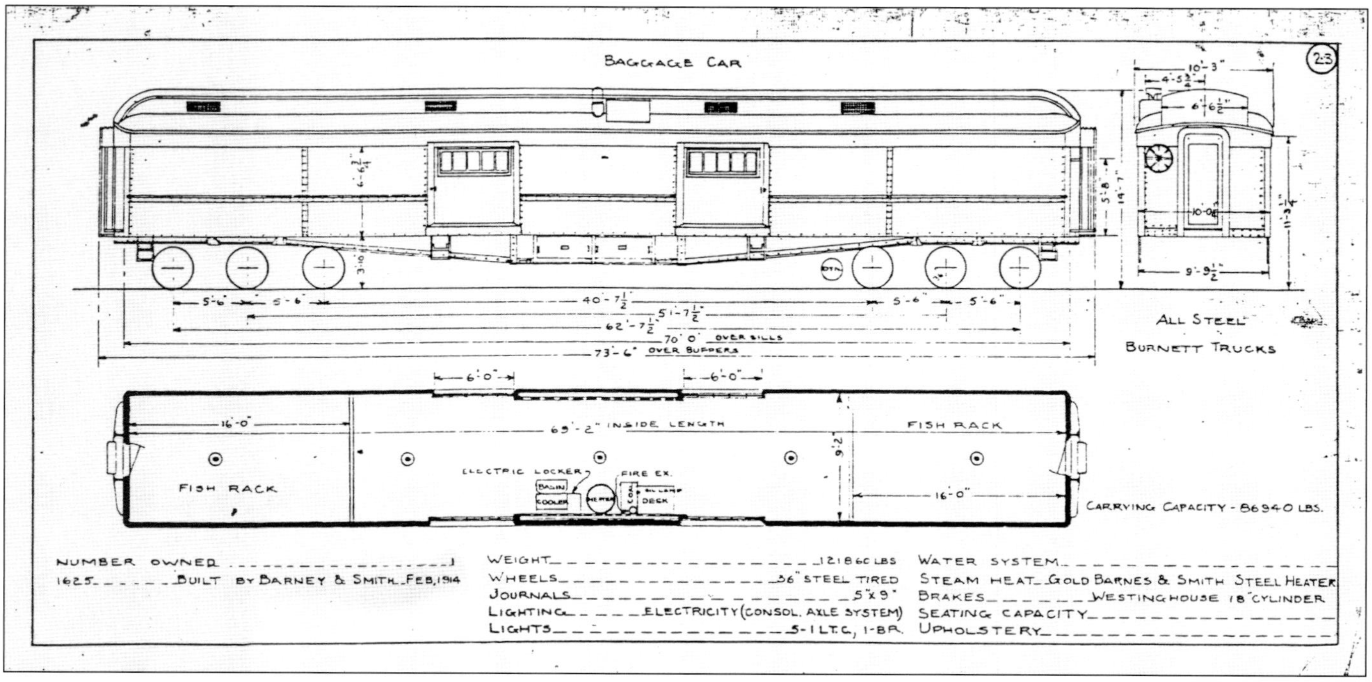

This Soo Line diagram illustrates a common example of the heavyweight baggage cars in the 70- to 75-foot length category. *Author's Collection*

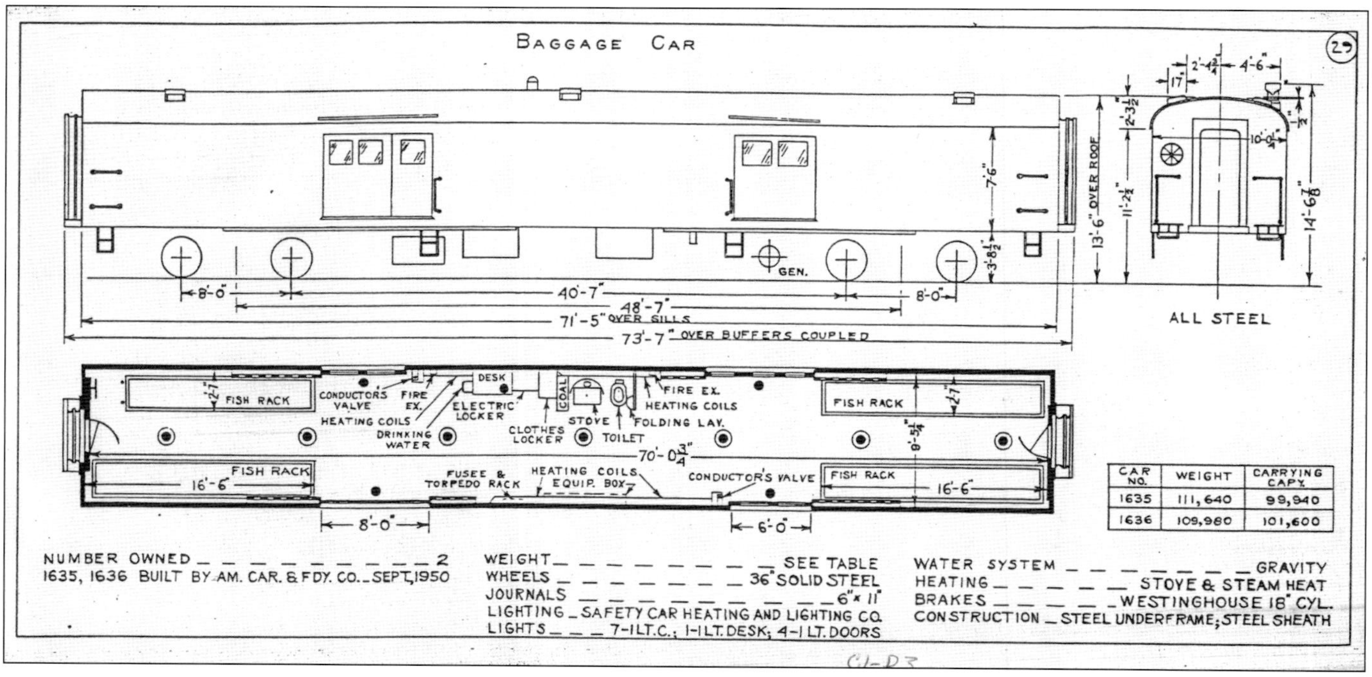

Soo Line streamlined baggage cars (1635 and 1636) illustrate a very common type of lightweight designs operated by many railroads.

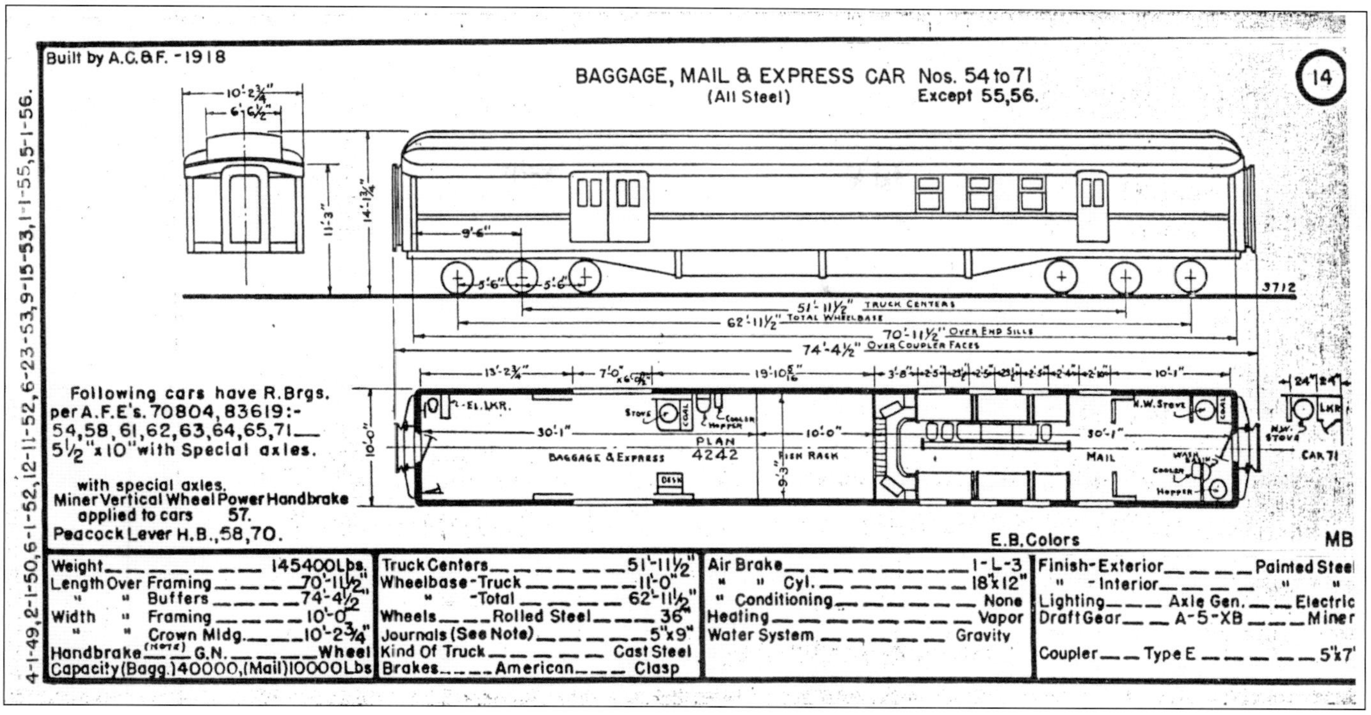

Many railway post office cars contained 30-foot space for the mail, plus a 40-foot section for baggage and express. *Soo Line Diagram, Author's Collection*

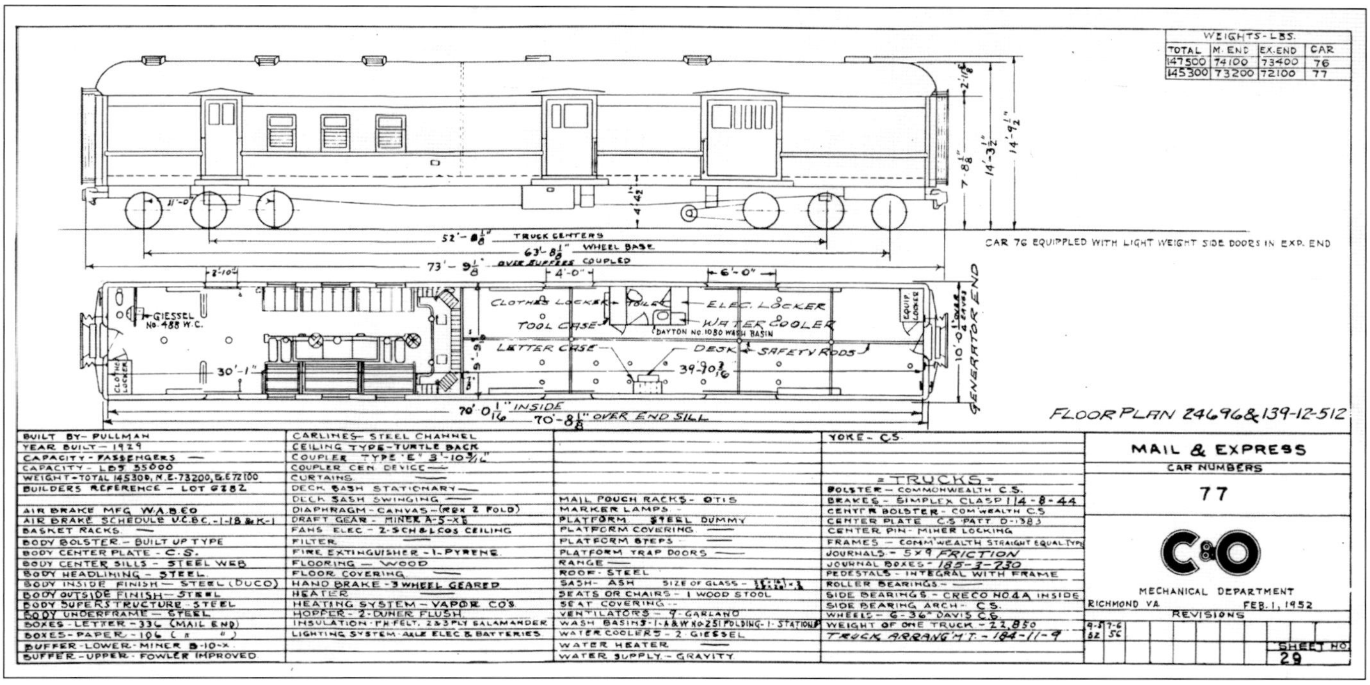

There were a number of RPO baggage cars with two sets of doors for the express and baggage section, such as this C&O car with 30-foot mail section, and nearly 40 feet of space for baggage and express. Note how the RPO sections are closed off from the remainder of the car. *C&O Diagram, Author's Collection*

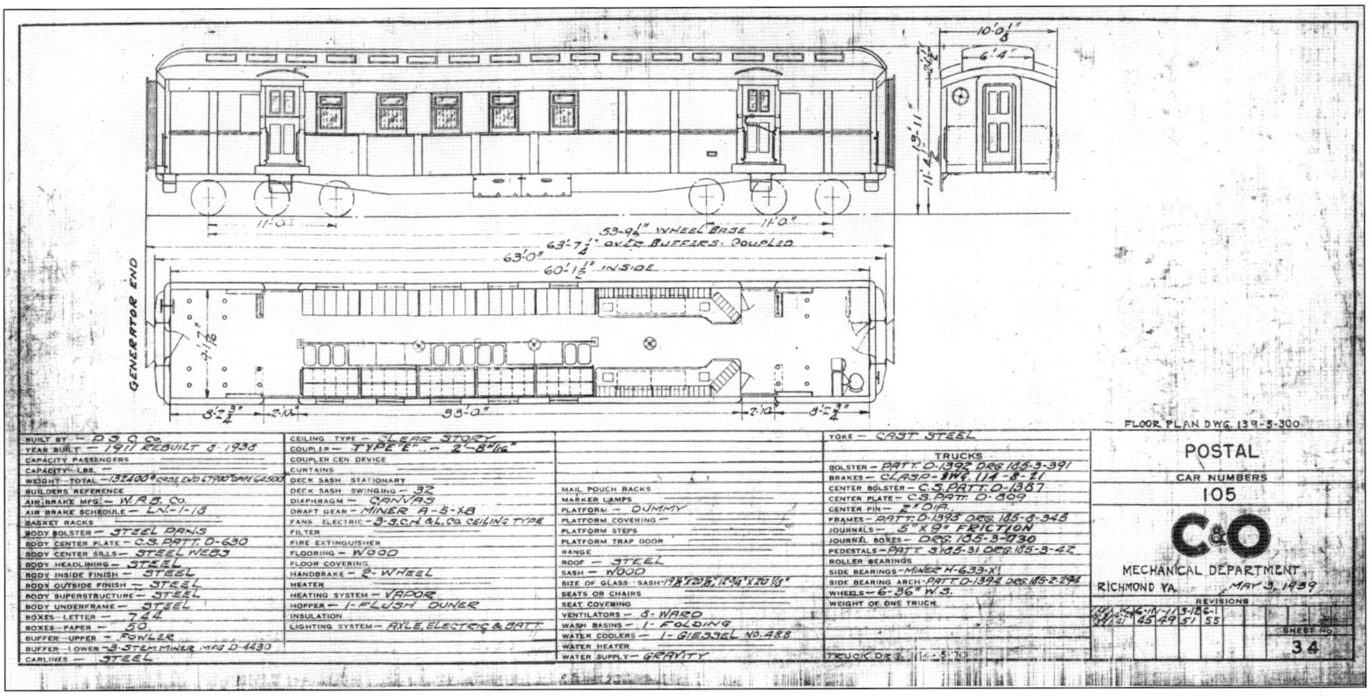

Some head-end equipment, both streamlined and heavyweight designs, were built exclusively for mail traffic. The cars contained a 60-foot section for the RPO with an overall length of 63 feet. This was true for both types of designs. *C&O Diagram, Author's Collection*

Southern Pacific baggage-express car #6008 and 6009 had a 40-foot inside length and were 43 feet, 6 inches long over the buffer. The equipment was operated primarily for express shipments as well as for baggage. This particular car is rather unusual as compared to most other types of head-end equipment since it quite short, and still in service in the mid-1940s. The 6008's portrait was taken in San Francisco in October 1946. The cars were still listed in the Official Register of Passenger Train Equipment in the early 1950s. *Harold K. Vollrath Collection*

Another example of a rather short head-end car is this Rio Grande railway post office-express car #60. The car was a narrow gauge car of wood construction, 46 feet long, and is shown here at Salida, Colorado, in June 1935. The Rio Grande owned two such cars, the other being #66. *Harold K. Vollrath Collection*

Burlington Route baggage car #1532 (1500 to 1591) is 74 feet, 3 inches long over the buffers. The car is marked for the Railway Express Agency. The car was photographed at Eola, Illinois, in February 1970. The car is still in the Pullman Green colors. *Owen Leander, William Raia Collection*

Chesapeake and Ohio baggage car #266 (264 to 270) is 73 feet, 9 inches long over the buffers. The car is painted in the C&O streamlined colors, and is shown here at Chicago in March 1970. *Owen Leander, William Raia Collection*

Another example of a baggage car painted in the streamlined colors is the Chicago and North Western's 8709 (8695 to 8709). The car is 64 feet, 3 inches long over the buffers. The car had just been recently pulled out of service. The car had been in express and mail service for many years and operated on such trains as the Duluth-Superior Limited. The car was in storage at Chicago in February 1968. *Owen Leander, William Raia Collection*

Burlington Route baggage car #998 (990 to 1054) was part of a streamlined group that was 79 feet, 2 inches long over the buffers. The silver car with black lettering is shown here at Chicago in April 1971—just one month before the advent of Amtrak. *Owen Leander, William Raia Collection*

C&NW's 85-foot baggage car #8902 (8900 to 8903) had an unusual placement for the loading doors. The car is out of service in this photo as it is July 1971, and Amtrak has begun full operations. Unfortunately the Chicago and North Western did not become part of the Amtrak Systems, even though it should have included the Chicago-Green Bay, Wisconsin corridor. *Owen Leander, William Raia Collection*

The Burlington Northern merger in 1970 resulted in the repainting of a number of passenger cars in the Cascade Green and White hockey stick scheme. Car #7025 is but one example of the repaints. It is shown here in Amtrak service at the new Midway Station for St. Paul-Minneapolis in the early 1970s. *Patrick C. Dorin*

Southern Pacific baggage car #6710 (6689 to 6764) was part of a group of cars purchased by the SP during the early to mid-1960s. The cars were 70 feet long and were painted only the grey color scheme. The car is shown here in Amtrak service at the old Great Northern depot in downtown Minneapolis in 1971. *Patrick C. Dorin*

The Burlington Route's Silver Pear, #450, was originally a baggage dormitory coach and was rebuilt as a full baggage car as illustrated here. The car was 88 feet, 8 inches long over the buffers. There was one other car in this group, the Silver Mesa #350. This portrait was taken in Chicago on April 10, 1971, about 3 weeks before Amtrak. *Owen Leander, William Raia Collection*

Burlington's Olympus, #907 (part of the 906 to 908 series), is another example of the streamlined baggage car fleet. This car was 72 feet, 3 inches long over the buffers. *Owen Leander, William Raia Collection*

One of the most common railway post office baggage cars was the 70-foot category (70 to 75 feet long depending on type of model) with a 30-foot Rail Post Office section—notice the area with the smaller door and three windows. St. Louis Southwestern, known as the Cotton Belt, #86 (79 to 89) is an excellent example of this type of equipment. Notice the placement of the lettering for the Post Office section and for the Railway Express Agency section. The car is shown here at Texarkana, Arkansas, in October 1948. *Harold K. Vollrath Collection*

Wabash #450, a Rail Post Office baggage car, had a 30-foot RPO section and 44 feet for the baggage and express. The car was 78 feet, 6 inches long and was one of two cars in the group, the other being #449. *Owen Leander, William Raia Collection*

Burlington's railway post office car #2330 (2320 to 2346) illustrates a typical example of the full 60-foot RPO car. Several railroads owned and operated such equipment. The 2330 has been repainted in the Burlington's silver colors to match the new streamliners. *William Raia Collection*

C&O's car #89 (81 to 91) has a 30-foot railway post office section as well as two doors for the express and baggage sections. The car is in the C&O streamliner colors of silver, blue and yellow. The car is shown here in service on C&O's Pere Marquette, train #11 at Grand Rapids, Michigan, after completing its run from Detroit. It is September 1969, and the Post Office has not yet discontinued mail service on the C&O. *Patrick C. Dorin*

Grand Trunk Western RPO baggage #8474 (8472 to 847C) was 66 feet, 8 inches long over the buffers. A similar type of car was also operated by the GTW's parent railroad, the Canadian National. The car is shown here in service at Chicago in July 1967. *William Raia*

Great Northern's 1107 (1105 to 1107) is a prime example of a streamlined RPO baggage car with a 30-foot railway post office section. The car is also marked for the Railway Express Agency. The 1107 is shown here at the head-end of the GN's Badger (from St. Paul) at Duluth, Minnesota, in the 1960s. The car is 85 feet long. *Patrick C. Dorin*

The Burlington's 85-foot car, Silver Post, has a 60-foot railway post office section, with approximately 15 feet for luggage or express shipments. The Burlington had one other car with this specific design, the Silver Page. Photographed in Chicago, April 1970. *Owen Leander, William Raia Collection*

Another example of the 85-foot RPO baggage with a 60-foot railway post office is the Illinois Central #1830 shown here at Chicago in April 1971. The car carries the final lettering design on regular passenger equipment before the advent of Amtrak. Note the new lettering to right with the new IC symbol. The words "railway post office" have been removed. The RPO services were just about completely finished by the end of the 1960s.

Minneapolis and St. Louis Railroad's GE-31 is a gas-electric self-powered car for handling short passenger trains. The car has a 30-foot railway post office and is shown here at Watertown, South Dakota, in June 1956. Note the consist of the train, which includes one streamlined coach and one baggage car. *Harold K. Vollrath Collection*

An example of a box express car, equipped with steam lines and high speed trucks, is the Canadian Pacific's #29114. The car is shown here in special train service on the Canadian Pacific (Soo Line) at Shoreham Yard (Minneapolis) in June 2004. Box express cars ranged in size from 40 feet to 50 feet, and were operated by many railroads throughout North America.

The Algoma Central operated head-end cars for express and baggage on its Sault Ste. Marie-Hearst, Ontario train services. AC's #301 is a former railway post office baggage car and was purchased from the Rio Grande Railroad. *Patrick C. Dorin*

The view illustrates the opposite side of AC's #301. *Patrick C. Dorin*

Express baggage car #308 is a former CN and VIA baggage car and operated on the trains to Hearst.

Chapter 2

COMBINATION PASSENGER – MAIL and BAGGAGE CARS

There was a wide variety of passenger equipment referred to as "combines."

Part of the car was generally designed for coach seating, while the remainder of the space was designed for baggage, express and even Rail Post Office service. The list of such equipment included such names as: coach-baggage, coach RPO-baggage, and coach-RPO. The combination cars could be observed on many types of trains, including commuter trains. In this case, the baggage section was often operated for the shipment of newspapers from the central city terminal, or even in some cases, mail bags destined for various suburban stations.

There was also a group of cars known as dormitory baggage cars. This type of equipment operated on variety of trains, but primarily on transcontinental trains (and even overnight trains) to provide sleeping accommodations for the food and beverage staffs and car attendants.

One of the interesting types of operations for the combination coach-baggage (and RPO space too in some cases), was the passenger service for mixed trains. A mixed train was a combination freight and passenger train. The combine was generally at the end of the train, and also served as a caboose for the train crew. The mixed train concept developed as automobiles took over more and more of the local train passenger loads. Thus the railroad was still able to provide some level of passenger service, even though the mixed freight and passenger train did not provide the same level of speed or reliability for on-time operations.

There were many types of combines ranging from 60-foot, standard heavyweight cars to 85-foot streamlined equipment, which also included the dormitory baggage cars.

The cars operated on many types of trains throughout North America. On the longer distance trains, the coach seating in the combines was often for passengers traveling shorter distances. The combines always followed the head-end cars in the train consist.

As a side note, sometimes the combine contained the only passenger seating for the entire train. This was often the case with dedicated mail and express trains, which could have anywhere from four head-end cars to as many as twenty-five.

The combination cars played an important role for many train services. In many cases, the cars also contained seating for the train crew plus a conductor's table for taking care of the passenger counts and other reporting for the particular schedule.

Combination cars were sometimes operated on "business car" trains to provide seating for the train crew, as well as the storage of materials that were to be provided for the freight customers, or for other reasons for the special train operation.

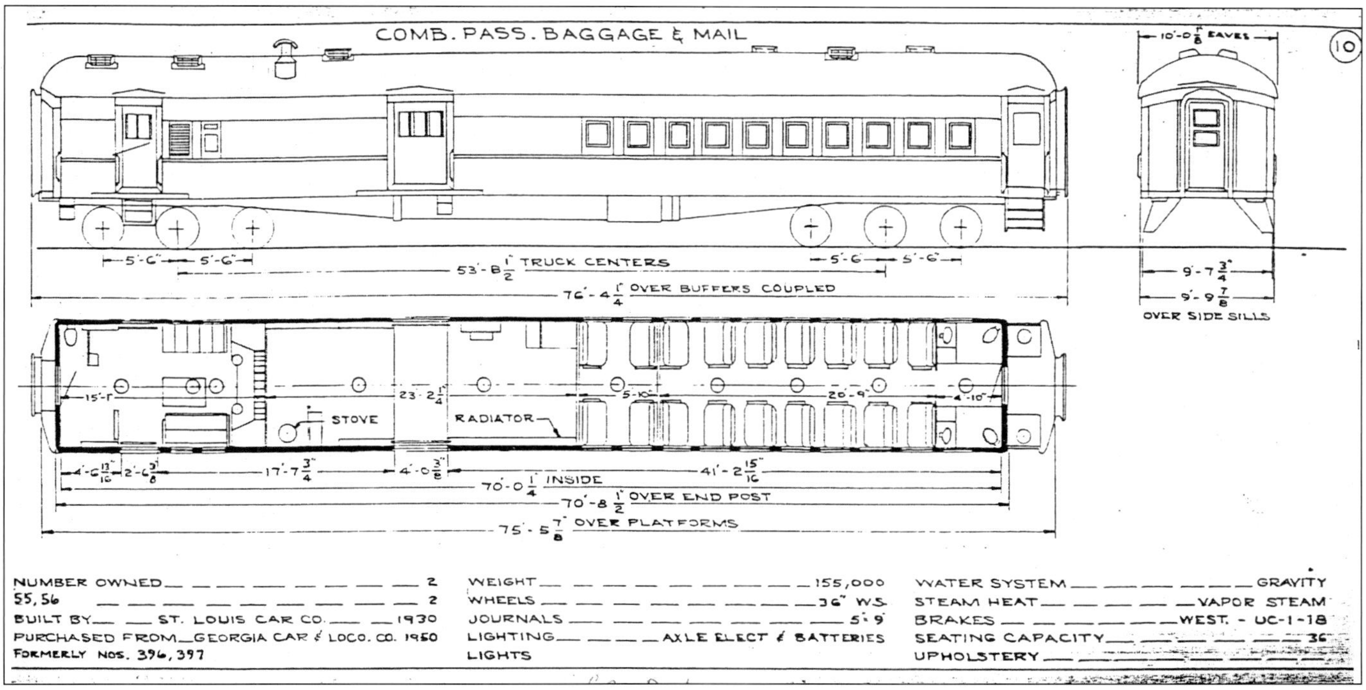

The Soo Line combination coach-baggage and RPO, numbers 55 and 56, are just one example of the heavyweight designs which included both the RPO and baggage section. Many combines contained only a baggage section as well as the coach seating. *Soo Line Diagram, Author's Collection*

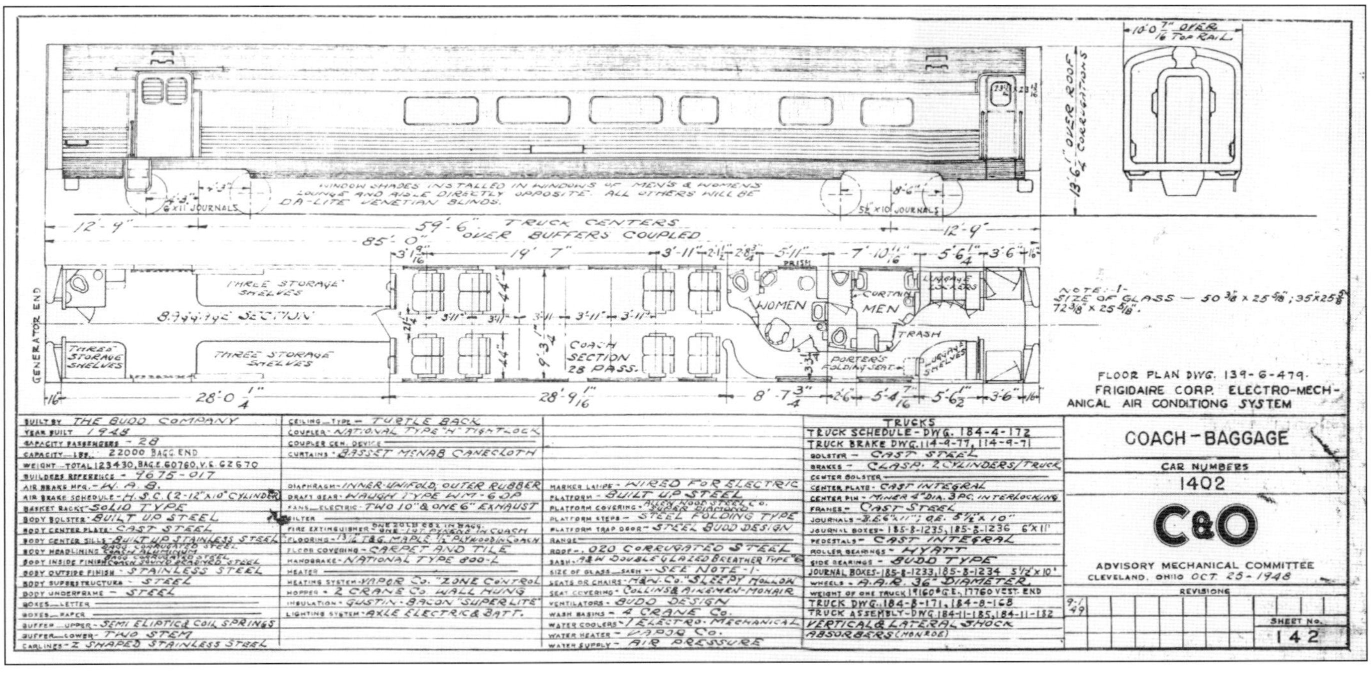

There were a number of streamlined or lightweight coach-baggage cars in service on many railroads. One example is this diagram of C&O streamlined car #1402. *C&O Diagram, Author's Collection*

Combination baggage-coach passenger equipment was used in a variety of train services. Not only were they a part of many consists of passenger trains, but were also used for mixed train services. Generally, the combines were placed at the rear of the train for both the train crew and passengers. Great Northern #566 (565 – 567) was 69 feet, 6 inches long over the buffers with a seating capacity of 40 passengers. GN's 566 is on the rear of a mixed train at Great Falls, Montana, in August 1949. *W. C. Whittaker Collection*

The Frisco combine #162 (and 166) were open end cars at the passenger end and were operated exclusively in mixed trains. Note the tank car ahead of the 56-foot car with a seating capacity of 30 passengers. The car is on the rear of the train which has stopped for switching for shippers at Springdale, Arkansas, in July 1939. *Harold K. Vollrath Collection*

Moving north to Alaska, combine #82 is part of a passenger train at Anchorage in July 1935. This particular car was purchased from the Southern Railway. *Harold K. Vollrath Collection*

Chicago and Western Indiana combine #40 was operated in commuter train service between Chicago and Dolton, Illinois. The car was often the single car consist for mid-day services. It had a 28-foot baggage section, a seating capacity of 48 passengers, and was 74 feet, 2 inches long over the buffers. *Photo by J. Buckley, William Raia Collection*

Northern Pacific's 1493 was a baggage -dormitory car. It was part of the 1493 to 1499 series. The car had a 41-foot baggage section and was 82 feet, 5 inches over buffers. *William Raia*

This Chicago and North Western combine's portrait was taken in February 1968. The number of the car is not visible and appears to have been painted out. The car may have been operated in commuter train services prior to the use of the new bi-level cars. The seating capacity may have been in the area of 72 passengers. *Owen Leander, William Raia collection*

The GM&O's combine #2594 had a seating capacity for 40 passengers plus the 25-foot baggage-express section. The car was 84 feet, 2 inches long and is shown here at St. Louis in October 1969. *William Raia*

The Milwaukee Road dormitory baggage car #1314 was part of the 1309 to 1316 series. The car was equipped with accommodations for 20 crew members, for the dining and lounge car staff as well as sleeping car and coach attendants. The car was 75 feet long. This equipment operated on the Olympian Hiawatha between Chicago and Seattle-Tacoma, as well as a crew car (sometimes) for the fast mail between Chicago and Minneapolis. *William Raia*

Gas-electric cars provided a substantial amount of train service on branch lines as well as main line local train operations. The Minneapolis and St. Louis GE-2 was a combination coach, baggage and railway post office car. The car carried the name "New Ulm," and is shown here at the Cedar Lake Shops of the M&St.L in Minneapolis in May 1948. *Jim Scribbins*

Boston & Maine gas-electric combine, #1182, was a combination coach and baggage car. It provided local train service for the B&M, and is shown here at Concord, New Hampshire, in July 1947. *Harold K. Vollrath Collection*

Gas-electrics were often used not only as combines, such as the Erie #5011, but for handling short local passenger trains. Including the gas-electric, a three-car consist is shown here at Waldwick, New Jersey, in April 1941. *Harold K. Vollrath Collection*

Chapter 3
COACHES and CHAIR CARS

Coaches generally followed the baggage and mail cars in the consists of most passenger trains. There was a wide variety of such equipment in operation during the many decades before Amtrak. And of course, much of the equipment continued to operate moving into the Amtrak era.

The variations of coach equipment included the standard heavyweight cars, the new streamlined cars and many innovations such as dome coaches, bi-level cars and the Santa Fe hi-liners, plus numerous variations of commuter equipment including electric multiple-unit cars and rail diesel cars.

The standard heavyweight cars could be divided into several groups. They varied in length from 60 feet to 80 feet in length. The seating capacity ranged from as few in the 50- to 60-seat range to as many as the 90s. It all depended upon the size of the car, and the types of service. The commuter cars and equipment that operated on local, short distance trains contained the highest number of seats.

The streamlined coaches, also known as "chair cars," were generally in the 85-foot long category. The seating capacity ranged from 44 for leg-rest seating to 60, up to 80, for equipment operated for short distance travel. The leg-rest cars were most often operated on transcontinental and overnight trains. The Canadian National even designated such equipment for the transcontinental and overnight operations as "day-nighters."

The streamlined cars were often equipped with dome seating where one could look up, down and all around. The dome coaches were operated primarily on railroads west of Chicago. However, the Baltimore and Ohio also operated dome coaches on some of the Chicago-Washington, D.C. train services.

Streamlined commuter equipment included both single level cars, some of which were electric multiple-unit, while others included the new bi-level or gallery cars. The latter could seat as many as 140 passengers depending upon the design.

There were a number of combination baggage - coach cars in both the standard heavyweight design and the streamlined cars.

The following photos illustrate some of the very interesting types of coach or chair car equipment operated by the railroads as well as Amtrak.

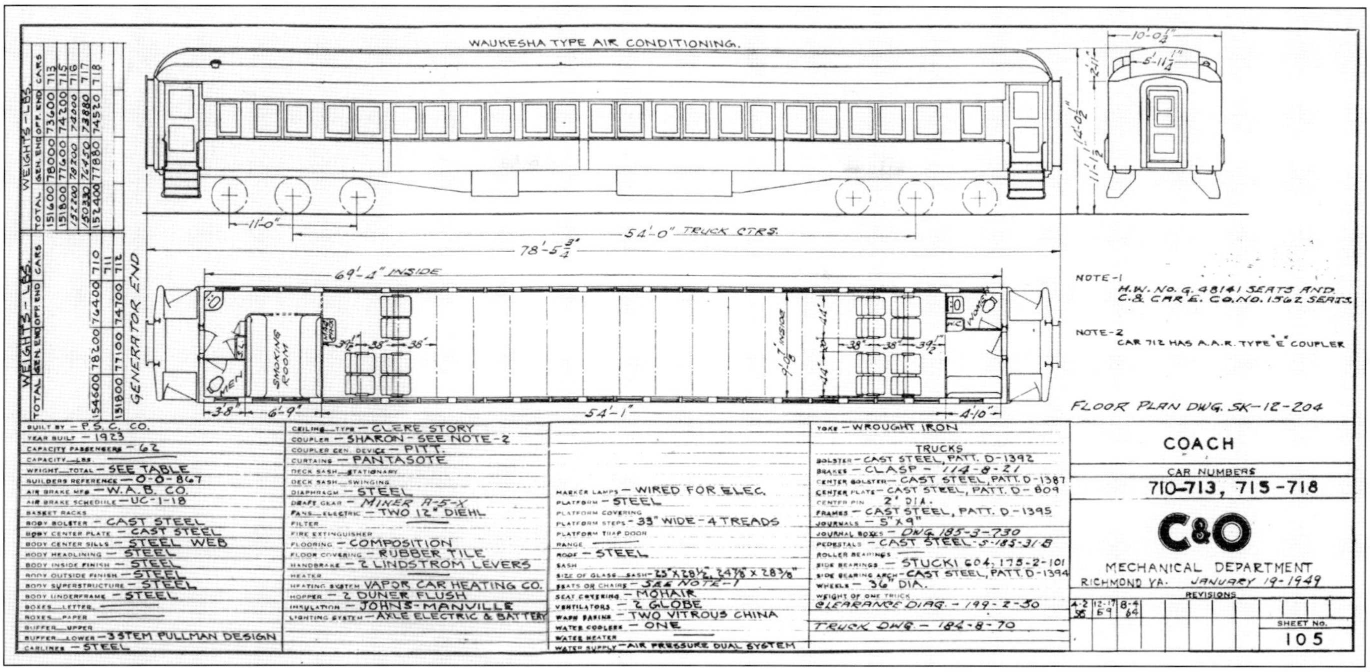

Standard heavyweight coach with a seating capacity of 62 passengers and an overall length of 78 feet, 5 3/4 inches. Standard coaches were constructed as short as 60 feet. *C&O Diagram, Author's Collection*

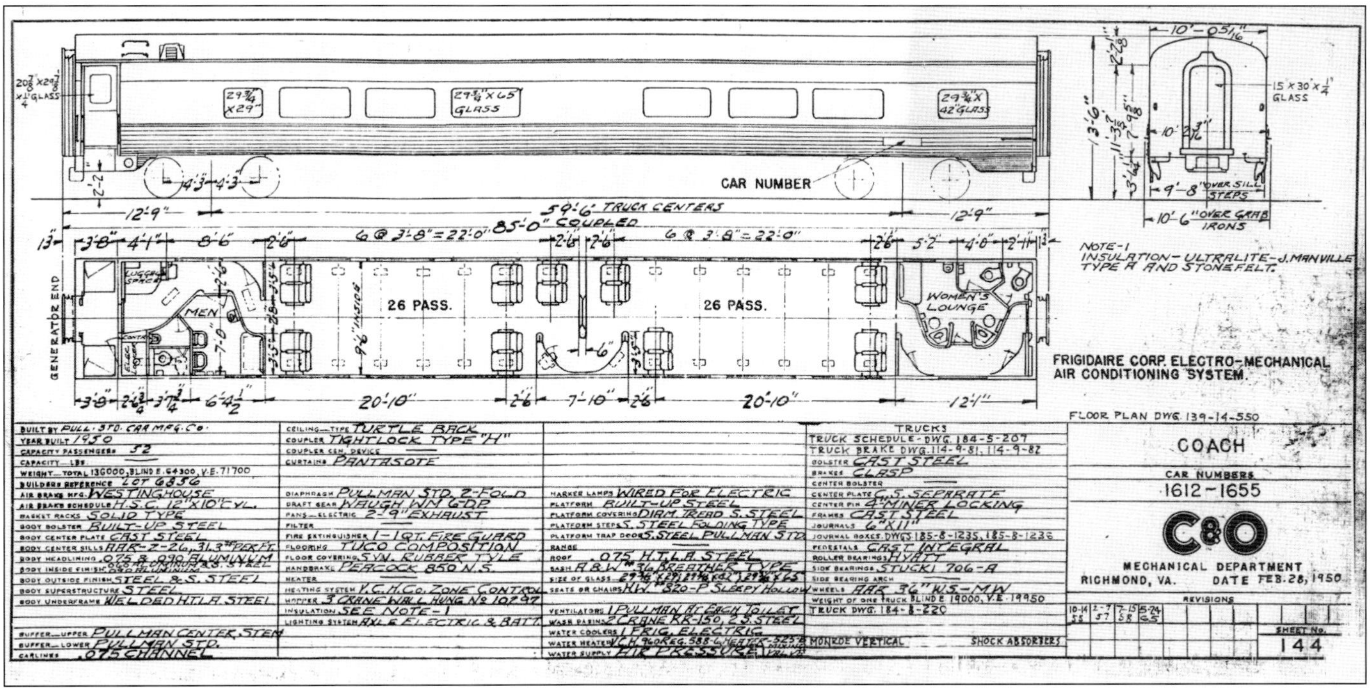

C&O streamlined coach is but one example of the types of lightweight equipment with an 85-foot length. Window configurations varied according the design by the individual railroads. *C&O Diagram, Author's Collection*

Burlington Route coach #6161 (6161 to 6168 & 6170) was a single window coach with a seating capacity of 83 passengers. The car was 79 feet, 8 inches long. The car once operated in some mainline services, but eventually may have been part of the commuter car fleet. *William Raia*

Duluth, Missabe & Iron Range Railway coach #33 (30 to 34) was part of a fleet of coaches operated on local passenger trains between Duluth and Hibbing, and Duluth and Ely, Minnesota. The seating capacity was 84 passengers and the length over buffers was 78 feet, 6 inches. It continues operation on the North Shore Scenic Railway between Duluth and Two Harbors as this is being written in 2010. *Patrick C. Dorin*

Grand Trunk Western's coach #5333 (5326 to 5333) had a seating capacity of 66 passengers and was painted in the CN's Maple Leaf color scheme of black and green with gold striping. The cars were 82 feet, 5 inches long. The 5333 was part of a Railroad Club of Chicago excursion trip in October 1966. *Jim Scribbins*

Santa Fe coach #1266 (1246 to 1295) had a seating capacity of 72 passengers, and was 78 feet, 3 inches long. The picture window arrangement for the coach seating was attractive, and the equipment was quite comfortable. *William Raia*

Still another version of the Santa Fe coaches was #1111 (1101 to 1121). This group had a seating capacity for 80 passengers and was 78 feet, 10 inches long. *William Raia*

Atlantic Coast Line coach #1118 (1116 to 1131) was an attractive rebuilt coach with seating for 56 passengers. Note the car has only one vestibule, which was common on the new streamlined passenger equipment. The car was 83 feet long. The car was photographed in Chicago on July 4, 1968, by Owen Leander. *William Raia Collection*

It is August 1955 at Russell, Kentucky, and C&O coach #823 (818 to 829) is what could be called a semi-streamlined car with the attractive C&O colors. This group had a seating capacity of 60 passengers and were 80 feet, 6 inches long. *William Raia*

Spokane, Portland and Seattle Railway streamlined coach #304 (301 to 305) was built by Pullman-Standard. The car was operated on the Western Star (and other trains) between Spokane and Portland. The seating capacity was 64 passengers and the cars were 85 feet long with a color scheme of dark green and gold striping. *Patrick C. Dorin Collection*

This photo SP&S 301 illustrates the opposite side of the 301 to 305 series. The car has been repainted with a wide gold stripe. The photo was taken in Chicago in the early 1970s. Note the Burlington bi-level commuter coach in the background to the right. *Patrick C. Dorin*

The Great Northern purchased a fleet of ex-400 Coaches from the Chicago & North Western. The cars were numbered 1076 to 1082, and 1086 to 1099. The cars were originally painted in the GN streamliner colors of orange and dark green, but later several received the Big Sky Blue. The seating capacity was 56 passengers and the length was 82 feet, 6 inches long. *Patrick C. Dorin*

Great Northern chair car #1116 (1110 to 1118) was part of the fleet originally operated on the Internationals between Seattle and Vancouver, British Columbia. The seating capacity was 60 passengers and the cars were 85 feet long. The car is shown here at Duluth in a North Shore Scenic Railway consist. *Patrick C. Dorin*

The Canadian Pacific purchased a fleet of streamlined coaches for operation on many of their trains, including the Mountaineer and the Soo-Dominion between St. Paul and Vancouver, British Columbia. Several of the cars were later sold to other railroads, such as the Algoma Central. In this case, the car is now part of the Canadian Pacific's passenger train fleet for special operations, and has been renamed. *Patrick C. Dorin*

It is August 1970 (less than a year to Amtrak) and L&N coach #3251 (3250, 3251) is shown here at Louisville, Kentucky. The cars had a seating capacity of 52 passengers and were 85 feet long. *Harold K. Vollrath Collection*

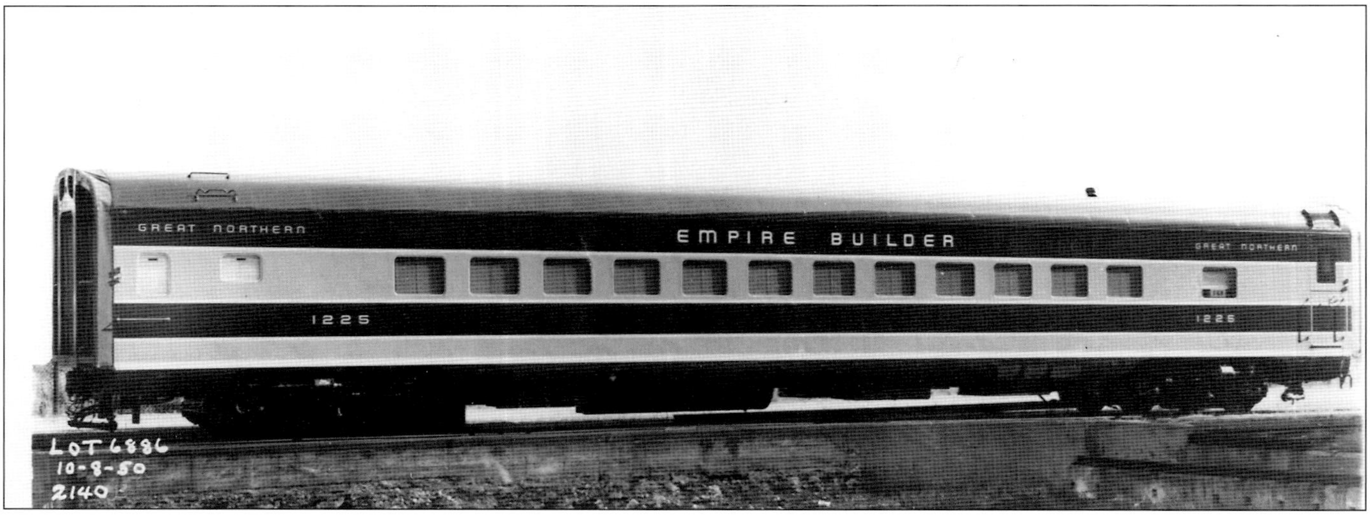

Great Northern day-night coach #1225 (1221 to 1232) was built for transcontinental service on the Empire Builder. Seating capacity was provided with 48 leg-rest seats. The cars were 85 feet long. *Pullman Standard Photo, Patrick C. Dorin Collection*

A number of the Kansas City Southern chair cars were named without visible numbers. This is the Port Arthur at Texarkana, Texas, in October 1952. *Harold K. Vollrath Collection*

Atlantic Coast Line chair car #236 was renumbered to 5415, the New Seaboard Coast Line number series 5408 to 5416. The car was 85 feet long and provided seating for 54 passengers. The car is shown here at Richmond, Virginia, in May 1969. *Harold K. Vollrath Collection*

Frisco coach #1257 (1250 to 1258) was named University City. The car was 85 feet long and provided seating for 56 passengers. The car is shown here on the rear of the Will Rogers, a daytime train between St. Louis and Oklahoma City. This photo by was taken at Newberg, Missouri, in May 1955. *Jim Scribbins*

C&O coach #1622 (1612 to 1655) provided seating for 52 passengers and was 85 feet long. The car is in service on one of the Pere Marquettes, train #11 (en route from Detroit to Grand Rapids) at Lansing, Michigan, in 1970. The consist of the train was simply just this one coach. *Patrick C. Dorin*

C&O coach #1618 illustrates the opposite side of the number series 1612 to 1655. This photo was taken in September 1969 at Grand Rapids, Michigan, and was part of a two-car train, a Pere Marquette, with a consist of one coach and one RPO-baggage car. *Patrick C. Dorin*

C&O coach #1637 illustrates the part of the rebuilding process on part of the fleet with the removal of the corrugated sides. *Owen Leander, William Raia Collection*

Canadian National heavyweight coach #5284 (5283 to 5307) had a seating capacity of 64 passengers and was 83 feet, 10 inches long over the buffers. In this October 1964 photo, the car is part of the Maple Leaf consist, a day schedule between Chicago and Toronto over the Grand Truck Western and the Canadian National. The car is shown here as the consist is moving into the Chicago Dearborn Station to be ready for the morning departure to Toronto. Note the CN's new color scheme black and a very light grey, nearly white, and is connected to a car with Maple Leaf scheme to the left of the photo. *Jim Scribbins*

This photo illustrates the interior of the leg-rest coach seating in one of the Great Northern dome coaches, which operated on the Empire Builder. The cars were decorated with Northwest Indian art. *Patrick C. Dorin*

The Algoma Central eventually purchased several Coaches from VIA, which were originally owned by the Canadian National. These two photos illustrate both sides of the coaches, which have operated on the Sault St. Marie-Hearst, Ontario train as well as the Agawa Canyon Tour Train. The cars were originally built in the mid-1950s, and have continued to operate in the 21st Century. *Patrick C. Dorin*

Close-up view of reclining seats, which in this case have been turned back-to-back to accommodate some table seating for special runs. Pull the level on the seat arm, push back and passengers were able to attain a new level of relaxation. *Patrick C. Dorin*

This view is of an interior of a 60-seat coach that once operated on the Great Northern's Internationals between Seattle and Vancouver, British Columbia. Note the window arrangement which was long enough for two sets of seats. *Patrick C. Dorin*

The interior of many coaches were equipped with the reclining seats arranged with a back-to-back position. *Patrick C. Dorin*

Passenger cars are equipped with a diaphragm at each end of the car for passengers to walk safely from one car to next. The cars also have safety gates that block the opening for use at the end of the train, such as can be observed with this photo of a meet between two passenger trains on the Algoma Central. *Patrick C. Dorin*

Chapter 4
COMMUTER COACHES

Commuter train operations are becoming more prominent and popular throughout North America after many decades of declining passenger patronage. The commuter train services throughout history, particularly through the 1970s, were provided with one of the greatest variety of coaches one could observe on the rail lines. Virtually each railroad had its own style of commuter coaches, although there were many similarities from one railroad to the next.

The seating, by the way, was flip-over seating or rotating seats for changing directions. This type of seating could be found in nearly all types of commuter cars. Reclining seats were not common on commuter equipment. However, there were a number of railroads that did offer a type of parlor car service for suburban passengers.

The Long Island Railroad was one in the New York City area, while the Chicago & North Western provided a similar type of service on certain runs in the Chicago area.

The types of Commuter Train Coaches include:

Electric Multiple Unit

The EMU cars were individual coaches that secure electric power, either through a pantograph on the roof reaching to the electric power wire; or through a electric pick-up shoe connecting to a third rail. Third rail type of equipment was common in the New York City area, such as the New York Central, while the overhead catenary was common on railroads in the Chicago area. However, there were many eastern railroads in the New York-New Jersey area with overhead wire.

The EMU equipment could be coupled together with consists ranging from two to perhaps as many as a dozen cars. The engineer in the lead car operated the trains over the designated route. Many of the EMU cars were also equipped with washrooms, but there were many without such accommodations. One example of equipment without washrooms was the Illinois Central with their older cars, which were eventually replaced by bi-level gallery cars which included washrooms. The Chicago, South Shore and South Bend Railroad, which operated on the Illinois Central in the state of Illinois, did have washrooms in their EMU cars.

Eventually, the EMU design was also adapted for streamlined commuter coaches, such as on the Chicago South Shore and the New Haven—not all at the same time period of course. The New Haven purchased some real interesting streamlined cars for operation in the New York area.

Diesel Multiple Unit

Beginning in the 1950s, the Budd Company produced self-propelled passengers equipment known as "rail diesel cars." Many railroads, such as the Boston and Maine, the Baltimore and Ohio, and the Pennsylvania Reading Seashore Lines operated the RDC cars for their commuter train operations.

Heavyweight Coaches

Many of the railroads purchased steel cars for their commuter rail services during the late teens and into the 1920s and 1930s. The number of orders, however, dwindled substantially as history moved forward throughout the 1920s, and into the Depression of the 1930s. As time went on, many of the railroad companies downgraded some of their long distance heavyweight coaches to commuter service. This included replacing the reclining seats with flip-over seating and expanding the seating capacity. This included placing seats in sections of the coach without windows.

Streamlined Coaches

As time went on, and many of the heavyweight coaches were aging, or were in need of heavy duty repairs, some of the railroads either gave up the services or purchased some streamlined equipment. This was the case on railroads such as the New Haven, the Rock Island and several others. The new streamlined cars were often equipped with the flip-over seats, or with all seating facing each other.

Bi-level Streamlined Coaches

In the late 1940s, railroads such as the Burlington Route invested in commuter equipment with the bi-level concept. There had been one or two designs of bi-level cars within the heavyweight categories, but the concept did not really take hold until the 1950s. Many of the Chicago railroads, such as the Rock Island, Chicago and North Western, the Milwaukee Road and the Southern Pacific in San Francisco, adopted the idea, which had been initiated in part by the Burlington Route.

The patronage on the commuter rail lines is reaching record levels and more as we move through the 21st Century. In fact, there are now more commuter rail lines in North America than there has been for the past 60 to 75 years. Most of the new services have purchased even newer designs of bi-level passenger equipment, such as the equipment placed in service on the GO Transit in Toronto during the 1970s.

Wabash coach #1234 (1233 to 1238) served in commuter service for the Wabash Railroad, and later the Norfolk and Western between Chicago and Orland Park. The Wabash car was painted in the company's blue color scheme with a silver roof. The seating capacity was 58 passengers, and the car length was 81 feet, 1 inch. The Wabash operated only one commuter train each way for the rush hour period. The route is now served by 15 trains each way during weekdays. *Jim Scribbins*

Pittsburgh and Lake Erie coach #431 (418 to 431) had a seating capacity of 64 passengers and was 79 feet, 2 inches long. The railroad initials are just above the number in the center of the car, while the words "New York Central System" are in the letter board. The car is in commuter train service at Pittsburgh, Pennsylvania, in this May 1958 photo. Unfortunately, there has not been any commuter train services in Pittsburgh for many years. *Harold K. Vollrath Collection*

Burlington Route coach 7127 (7100 to 7166) is another example of commuter service equipment. The seating capacity was 96 passengers. The car was in full service in July 1965 when this photo was taken. At that time, the car could have been part of Burlington commuter train consists with the new bi-level cars, which at that were steam heated. *William Raia Collection*

The Burlington operated several semi-streamlined commuter cars such as the 4525 (4520 to 4526). The seating capacity was 64 passengers with a length of 79 feet, 9 inches. The car was photographed in service at Eola, Illinois, on February 28, 1970, just two months before the Burlington Northern merger. *Owen Leander, William Raia Collection*

Going back to the 1940s (June 6, 1940 in this case), the C&NW operated a number of cars in commuter that were in the 60-foot long category. Car #3084 was 69 feet long over the buffers and had a seating capacity of 78 passengers. The number series was 3000 to 3086. *William Raia Collection*

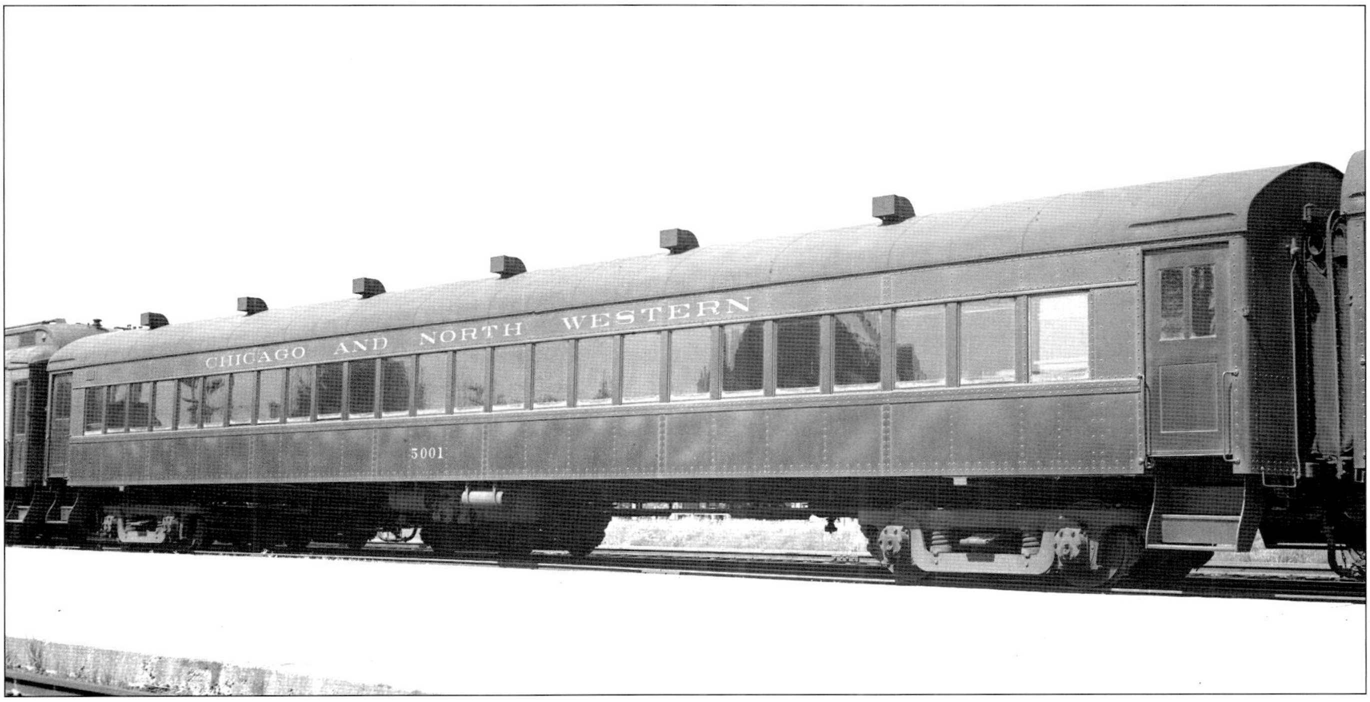

The Chicago & North Western also operated a fleet of semi-streamlined cars, such as 5001 (5000 to 5123). The seating capacity was 96 passengers and the cars were 81 feet long. This car appears to be in the same consist as the C&NW 3084 illustrated previously—the exact same date of June 6, 1940. *William Raia Collection*

The C&NW followed the Burlington's example with new bi-level (or gallery) commuter cars. Car #39 was part of the 17 to 48 number series and had a seating capacity of 161 passengers. At first the cars were heated by steam generator equipped motive power, but were later re-equipped with head-end power from F-7s equipped with generators. The 33's portrait was taken in August 1969 at Barrington, Illinois. The cars were 85 feet long. *William Raia*

Rail diesel cars are self-powered equipment and were designed and constructed by the Budd Company during the 1950s. There were a number of cars built for intercity service, but a sizeable fleet operated in commuter train service. Here is a two-car train on the Central Railroad of New Jersey at Jersey City in October, 1964. The lead car number is 557 and was built by Budd in 1955. *Harold K. Vollrath Collection*

The Chicago, South Shore and South Bend Railroad, and many other companies such as the Pennsylvania, the Illinois Central and the New Haven operated EMU coaches for commuter service. South Shore car #23 was a rebuilt coach with picture windows. The South Shore cars were orange with maroon letter boards and silver roofs. The 23 is shown here at Gary, Indiana, in January 1973. *Patrick C. Dorin*

Seating for commuter accommodations were (and are) flip-over seats—the back of chair could easily be pushed to the other side of the seat cushion. This interior photo illustrates the seating for a heavyweight coach. *Patrick C. Dorin*

This interior of a gallery commuter car illustrates the flip-over single seating at the upper level. The seating at the lower level accommodated two passengers. *Patrick C. Dorin*

Chapter 5
PARLOR CARS

The parlor car concept dates back to at least the early part of the 20th Century. The cars provided first class accommodations with single reclining seats, which were often able to rotate. It was a step up from the coach seating. Most of the cars were equipped with single seats on each side. However, there were some designs with single seating on one side with double seating on the other side.

Parlor cars came in a variety of styles. Generally, the cars were similar to coaches, but many were combination parlor lounge cars, or parlor observation cars.

In some cases, parlor cars were designed with a buffet at the front, 2 or 4 sets of table seating, then the parlor car seating with observation windows at the rear of the car.

Parlor car equipment in operation included both heavyweight cars and streamlined cars throughout the 1940s into the late 1960s, and even the early 1970s.

For many years, the Parlor cars were part of the Pullman Company operations.

Color schemes ranged from the Pullman Green color with the word "Pullman" in the letter board to the railroad company color schemes. The lettering for the individual railroad colors included either simply the word "Pullman" or the railroad name in the letter board. When the railroad name was in the letter board, the word "Pullman" was generally in small lettering in the upper corners of the car sides.

Moving into the streamliner era, the Pullman Company participated less as time went on with the operation of the parlor cars. That being the case, only the railroad name was in the letter board.

The parlor car designation began changing gradually in the late 1960s to such words as "club cars." Eventually, into the Amtrak era the wording became known as the "business class."

Parlor cars were a comfortable daytime way to travel, especially if the car was a combination observation lounge or even with a buffet or dinette. Depending upon the type of train, the number of parlor cars could range from only one to as many as three or four. This chapter reviews the different types of parlor cars and the seating arrangements.

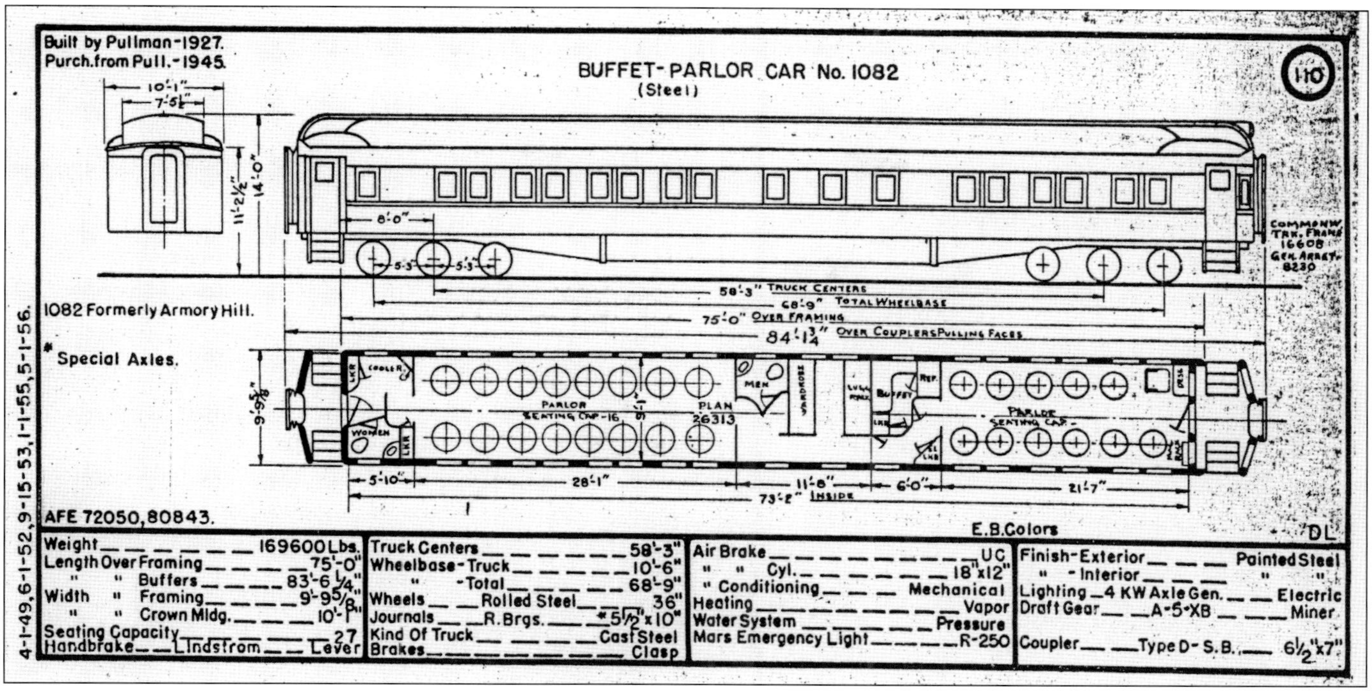

Parlor cars provided single seating on rotating, reclining chairs. Parlor cars came in a variety of designs, both in the heavyweight standard era as well as the streamlined era. It all depended upon the individual railroad's needs. This is a Great Northern Railway parlor car equipped with a buffet section. This particular design also had a red Mars light at the rear of the car, and was generally operated as the last car in the train's consist. *GN Diagram, Author's Collection*

It is August 1946; and the Monon Railroad would soon be acquiring streamlined cars, many of which were rebuilt types of equipment. The company owned one parlor car, the 110, in the mid-1940s. The car operated in the Chicago-Indianapolis train service. The car was off the roster by the early 1950s. Note the Monon wording in the letterboard, and the CI&L initials in the upper corners of the car. Many railroads operated heavyweight parlor cars, many of which were part of the Pullman fleet. *Harold K. Vollrath Collection*

The Grand Trunk Western parlor, the Michigan, is an example of an older style car. Note the truss rods at the bottom of the car. This photo shows the steel plating and an earlier GTW insignia without the maple leaf. The car is not air-conditioned either. This photo was taken at South Bend, Indiana, with the car on the rear of a Railfans Special on July 21, 1940. *R. Kennedy, William Raia Collection*

The Pullman parlor car, the Mill Creek, is in the typical color scheme of "Pullman Green," used on Pullman cars for many decades. In fact, many of the Pullman sleepers carried the green into the early 1960s, although many had been repainted in a particular railroad's streamliner colors. The Mill Creek is shown here at South Boston, Massachusetts, on October 12, 1946. The car was operating in service for the New Haven Railroad. The Mill Creek had 28 parlor car seats and 1 drawing room. *William Raia*

The Milwaukee Road parlor car, the Wisconsin Valley, #191, was originally in the orange and maroon scheme, but was repainted in the Union Pacific colors during the late 1950s. This took place after the UP streamliners were transferred from the Chicago and North Western to the Milwaukee Road. The seating capacity of the Valley Series parlor cars was 35 passengers. The car is shown here at Chicago on June 27, 1971, and Amtrak was already underway utilizing Milwaukee Road equipment. *Owen Leander, William Raia Collection*

Great Northern parlor vars #1083 and 1084 were rebuilt cars from heavyweight cars. The cars received streamlined roofs, picture windows and a short buffet section near the front of the car. Although the rear wall of the car had windows, it did not have observation car seating at the rear of the train. The cars were named the Twin Cities and the Twin Ports, contained seating for 26 passengers and were 83 feet, 6 inches long. Note the diaphragm at the rear of the car. The car is at the rear of the Gopher departing Duluth for St. Paul with an 8-car consist in April 1968. *Patrick C. Dorin*

Gulf, Mobile and Ohio parlor car #2107 (2106 to 2109) was 85 feet long, and had a seating capacity for 31 passengers. The car ran on six-wheeled trucks. The name of #2107 was "Springfield." *Patrick C. Dorin*

GM&O parlor car #5931 (and 5930) had a similar window arrangement (but not identical) to Chicago & North Western "400" type coaches. The 5930 and 5931 also had riveted sizes and had kept the wide diaphragms at the end of the cars. This was rather unusual to see in 1970, when this photo was taken at Chicago. *Owen Leander, William Raia Collection*

Amtrak parlor car #3770 was the former Great Northern parlor observation car, the Port of Seattle, car #1195. The car was originally part of the Internationals, a set of streamliners between Seattle and Vancouver, British Columbia on the GN. The GN owned and operated two cars for the International fleet, the other being #1196, the Port of Vancouver. The cars were 85 feet long. The car became part of the Amtrak fleet in 1971, and operated for a while on the Twin Cities Hiawatha—shown here at the old Great Northern Station in Minneapolis. The car was sold in 1977. *Patrick C. Dorin*

Parlor cars provided single, rotating reclining seats for "First Class Daytime Travel." This photo shows the interior of the former Great Northern parlor car, #1195, the "Port of Seattle." The car had a total seating capacity for 29 passengers including a drawing room. The rear of the car contained seating toward the observation windows. It was a great way to view the railroad line as well as the passing scenery. *Patrick C. Dorin*

Chapter 6
DINING and LOUNGE CARS

The food and beverage service cars were often a drawing card for repeat passengers. There were not only full dining cars, but combination dining lounge cars (sometimes known as café lounge cars) and full lounge cars, sometimes known as club lounge cars. Furthermore, the lounge cars were often designed as observation lounge cars either as a full lounge car service, but also in combination with sleeping car accommodations or parlor car seating.

The new streamlined cars often had the same type of food and beverage facilities as the standard heavyweight cars. However, there were a number of new innovations. Some examples include the dome dining cars on the Union Pacific, and the dome lounge cars built for several western railroads. The dome lounge cars were built with several configurations. Some were dome lounge observations cars, with others designed for mid-train operations. These included both short dome as well as full dome cars. There were several types of full dome cars that had been built for the Milwaukee Road, Santa Fe, and the Great Northern.

Dining and lounge cars were often designed as combination cars with sleeping, parlor and/or coach accommodations. The Soo Line referred to such equipment as sleeper restaurant lounge cars. A combination car with a coach seating was often called a café lounge coach. However, there were many more types of names for the various designs found on each and every railroad line.

The standard heavyweight cars ranged in size from about 75 feet to 80 feet in length. The streamlined cars were generally in the 85-foot category.

It should be mentioned that often the food and beverage cars were given special names. Lounge cars built for the Northern Pacific's North Coast Limited were known as the "travelers rest". Coffee shop cars on the Great Northern's Empire Builder were known as "ranch cars." Still other designations of food and beverage cars included the terms: tavern car, tavern club lounge, tap-café lounge, buffet lounge, and bar lounge cars.

The design of the equipment, as well as the service, played a major role in the popularity of many passenger trains. As mentioned above, the design and service levels were part of the selling point for the use of comfortable passenger train travel.

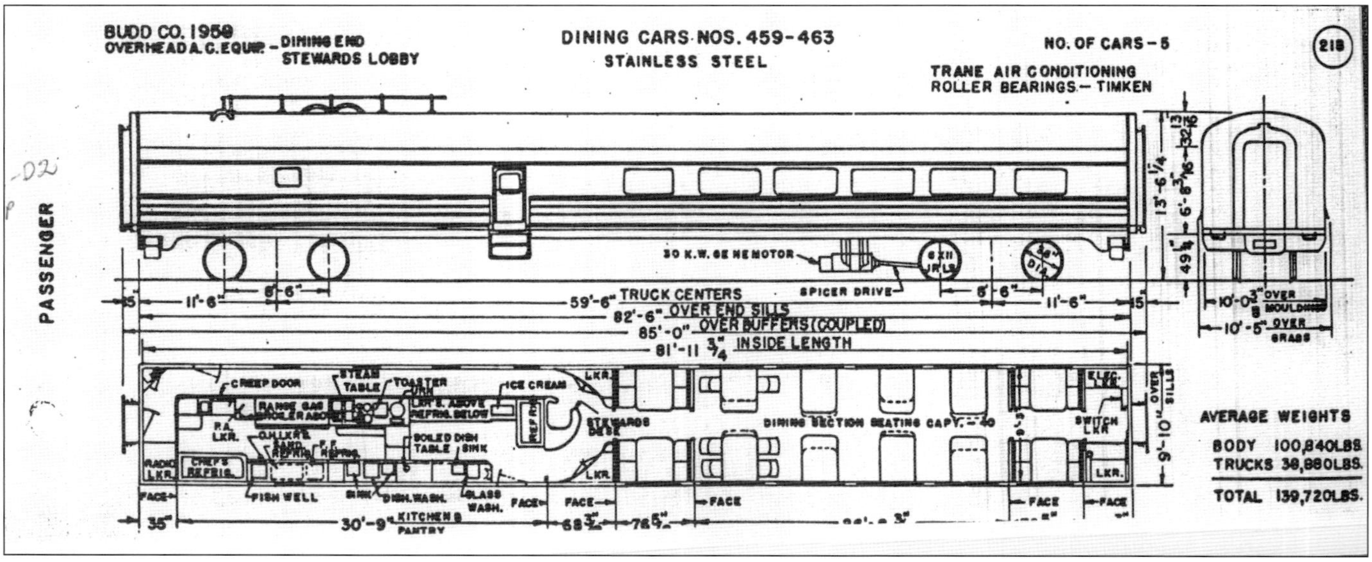

Streamlined, lightweight dining cars were generally 85 feet long and had 6 windows on each side of the dining room.
Northern Pacific Diagram, Author's Collection

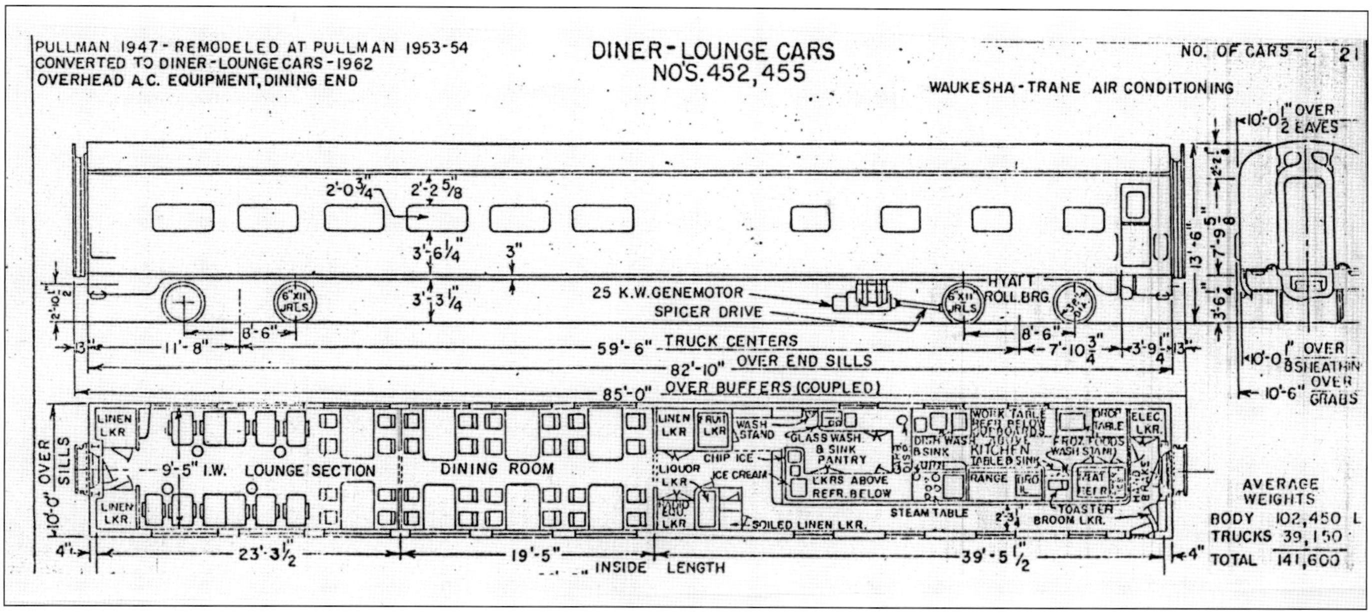

Café lounge or diner-lounge cars were designed for shorter passenger trains with the objective to provide both lounge and dining areas for the passengers. This streamlined car is the typical 85-foot length, whereas the heavyweight cars were in the 70- to 80-foot lengths. *Northern Pacific Diagram, Author's Collection*

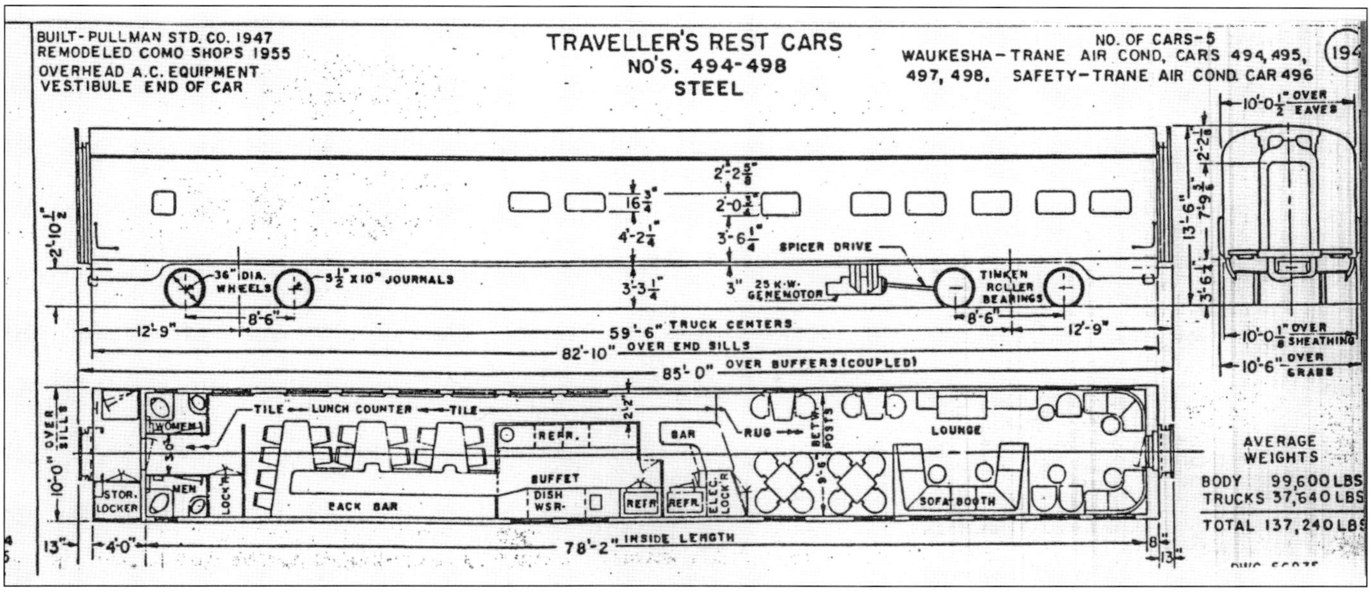

Many food and beverage cars were designed to provide a new and inviting atmosphere to attract passengers, and to provide lower cost meals as compared to the general dining car menus. The Northern Pacific's traveler's rest cars are just one example. *Northern Pacific Diagram, Author's Collection*

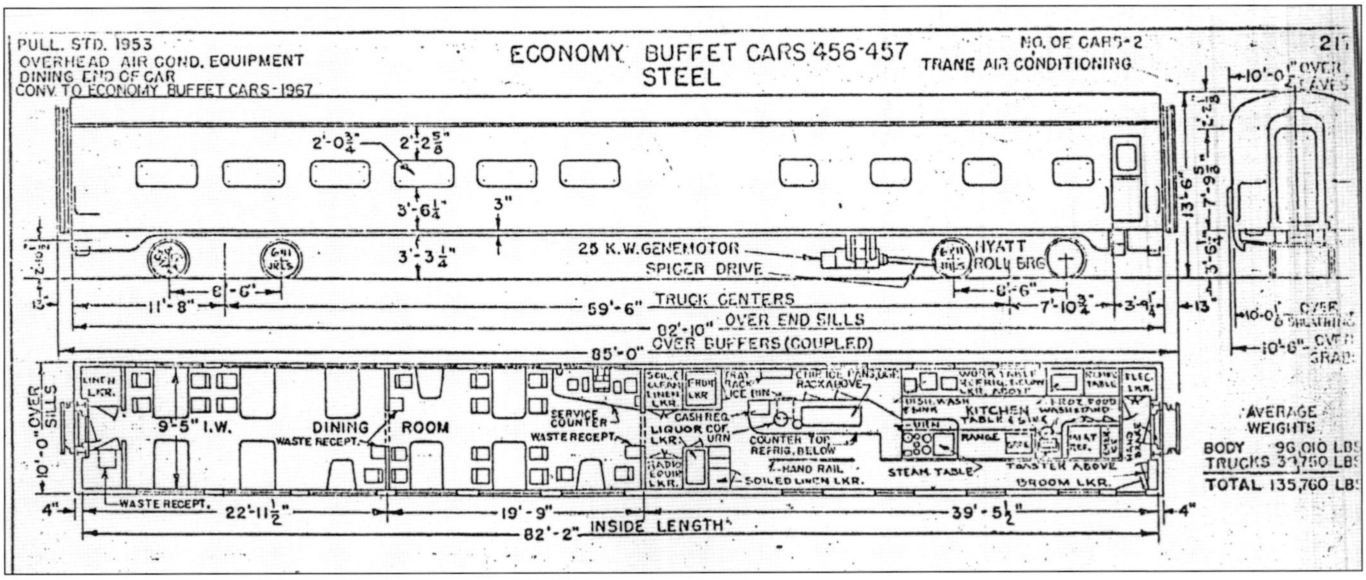

The NP also created an economy buffet car for operation on their secondary transcontinental trains, such as the Mainstreeter. *Northern Pacific Diagram, Author's Collection*

Chicago and North Western dining car #6934 was part of the 6932 to 6935 series. The car had a seating capacity in the dining room for 36 passengers. Six tables provided seating for 4 passengers, while the six others accommodated 2 passengers. This car is lettered for Treasure Island Special, while the number of the car and the C&NW initials are in the center below the windows. The photo of the car was taken at Berkeley, California, in September 1939. *W. C. Whittaker*

This C&NW dining car is painted in a two-tone grey scheme for operation in the Overland Limited, a joint C&NW-UP through transcontinental train service. The 6917 provided seating for 46 passengers and was 82 feet, 1 inch long. This was a C&NW photo. Note the difference in the types of windows for the dining room areas of the two C&NW dining cars. *Jeffrey M. Koeller Collection*

This Rio Grande Railroad dining car was of wood construction, and was eventually converted to work car service. The car number was X-3272 and was designated a kitchen-diner-sleeper. The car is shown here at Grand Junction, Colorado, in March 1947. *Harold K. Vollrath Collection*

Gulf, Mobile and Ohio dining car #1073 (1073 to 1076) is a good example of a heavyweight car repainted in the streamliner colors. The dining room provided seating for 44 passengers. The cars were 83 feet, 2 inches long over the buffers. The car is shown here in service on a Chicago-St. Louis trip at Joliet, Illinois, in July 1969. *William Raia*

The Soo Line rebuilt two coaches (former 2013 and 2017) into dining club lounge cars for service on the Laker between Chicago and Duluth, Minnesota. The cars had a total seating capacity of 32 passengers for the dining and lounge sections. The cars were 73 feet, 9 inches long over the buffers. The 2017, shown here, was on display at North Freedom, Wisconsin, in August 1992. This equipment was listed as dining parlor car in equipment registers. *William Raia*

Great Northern dining car #1032 was a rebuilt car and is riding on the original six-wheel trucks. The car had a rebuilt streamlined roof as well as picture windows and more, and was 83 feet, 4 inches long, shown here on the rear of the Badger at Superior, Wisconsin, in January 1967. The dining room had seating for 46 passengers. *Patrick C. Dorin*

C&O's lunch counter lounge car #1922 (1920 to 1922) provided seating for 32 folks in the dining area, and 10 in the tavern lounge area. The car also contained rear windows as well as a diaphragm. Thus, the car could operate conveniently either as the last car or somewhere in the middle of the consist. The car was photographed at Chicago in June 1970. Note the C&NW commuter car to the right. *Owen Leander, William Raia Collection*

C&NW club lounge car #7902 (7901) was part of the North Western's two-car fleet, which was originally part of the transcontinental streamliner sets with the Union Pacific. The car had a seating capacity for 36 passengers. The car is shown here in its final color scheme of yellow and green, with yellow lettering and black numbers. The car was still in active service in February 1968. *Owen Leander, William Raia Collection*

This photo illustrates the opposite side of the C&NW 7902. *Owen Leander, William Raia Collection*

The C&NW converted some of the food service cars with higher roof to match the size of the new bi-level 400s that went into service in the late 1950s. Car #6953 (6954) is shown here with its high roof. The car had a seating capacity in the dining room for 56 passengers. This photo was taken in March 1970 at Chicago. *William Raia*

The Burlington named many of their streamlined cars. This California Zephyr dining car carried the name "Silver Café." The car is shown here at Chicago just prior to Amtrak, beginning in May 1971. *Owen Leander, William Raia Collection*

Cars not assigned to the California Zephyr simply carried the name "Burlington." They were also named, such as the dining car "Silver Manor," shown here at Minneapolis. The cars provided seating for 48 passengers. *Owen Leander, Willaim Raia Collection*

Canadian Pacific dining car, the Frontenac, was one of a fleet of 18 dining cars built by the Budd Company for the Canadian and the Dominion. The dining room provided seating for 48 passengers. The car is shown here at Calgary, Alberta, on one of the transcontinental Montreal-Toronto and Vancouver trains in October 1966. *William Raia*

This Great Northern Railway photo illustrates the type of table seating (in this case four at each table) that was very common in dining cars for many decades, and still is to this day on some of the Amtrak equipment. *Lake Superior Railroad Museum Collection*

This Milwaukee Road photo from the late 1920s illustrates the interior of a lounge car which operated on the Pioneer Limited between Chicago and St. Paul-Minneapolis. *Author's Collection*

This interior photo of the Great Northern's ranch car illustrates the lounge section of the coffee shop lounge which operated on the Empire Builder. *Great Northern Photo, Lake Superior Railroad Museum Collection*

Dining car interiors were equipped with table seating, which included the linen, silverware, and quite often a display of flowers. *Amtrak*

The ranch car menu on the Great Northern's Empire Builder. *Author's Collection*

Meal service equipment could be equipped with square or rectangular tables as well as tables of different designs with angle seating adjacent to the windows. This interior view is an Amtrak car, which was a former Great Northern coach-diner originally constructed for the Internationals between Seattle and Vancouver. This type of seating was a drawing card for passengers. There were many dining and lounge cars with the variety of table and seating designs. *Patrick C. Dorin*

Chapter 7
SLEEPING CARS

Sleeping cars operated on the overnight trains and the transcontinental services. The Pullman Company was the primary operator of the equipment for the many railroads offering passenger train service. Some railroads, such as the Soo Line, often operated their own sleeping cars as well as having Pullman-operated cars on the line.

The standard heavyweight sleeping cars were painted primarily in the Pullman Green color with gold lettering. However, as the new streamlined sleeping cars were beginning to enter service, they were painted in the participating railroads' colors. For example, one could observe a streamlined sleeping car with the railroad name in the letter board, with the word Pullman in smaller lettering, either on the upper corners of the car or below the window line adjacent to the entry doors. However, the reverse was also true with the name Pullman in the letter board, with the railroad name in smaller letters.

The seeping car accommodations contained a variety of designs. There were the upper and lower berths, roomettes, single and double bedrooms, compartments and drawing rooms. The Pennsylvania Railroad even included what was called a master bedroom. Many of the individual rooms had their own toilet facilities. Passenger riding in the open sections (the upper and lower berths) had access to full washroom and dressing room facilities at the end of the car.

The number of types of sleeping cars was immense with both the standard heavyweights and the streamlined cars. Some sleeping car designs were combination cars with dining and lounge facilities. Examples of the various types are as follows:

Standard Heavyweight Equipment

16 sections, tourist
14 sections, tourist
12 sections, 1 drawing room
10 sections, 1 drawing room, 2 compartments
8 sections, 1 drawing room, 2 compartments
6 sections, 6 double bedrooms
12 roomettes, 2 single bedrooms, 3 double bedrooms

Streamlined Cars

16 duplex roomettes, 4 double bedrooms
6 sections, 6 roomettes, 4 double bedrooms
10 roomettes, 6 double bedrooms
6 roomettes, 3 bedrooms, buffet-lounge
10 roomettes, 3 double bedrooms, 2 compartments
4 compartments, 4 double bedrooms, 2 drawing rooms

The sleeping cars generally followed the food and beverage cars in the consist of overnight trains. However, this was not always the case. Consists varied according to the type of train and the service levels. There were also all-Pullman trains, such as the Santa Fe's Super Chief and the Pennsylvania Railroad's Broadway Limited.

Overnight trains were very convenient for business travel. A person could board the train in the late afternoon, or even later in the evening, and travel overnight to the destination while getting a good night's sleep. The next morning, the person could go to the scheduled meeting or other business activities. When completed, in the afternoon the individual could return to depot and catch the train overnight back home. It was a relaxing way to travel, and one had time to think, read, or even have some interesting conversations with other passengers.

Passengers can still enjoy sleeping car service on the Amtrak trains as we roll through the early part of the 21st Century.

The following illustrates the types of Pullman sleeping car accommodations.

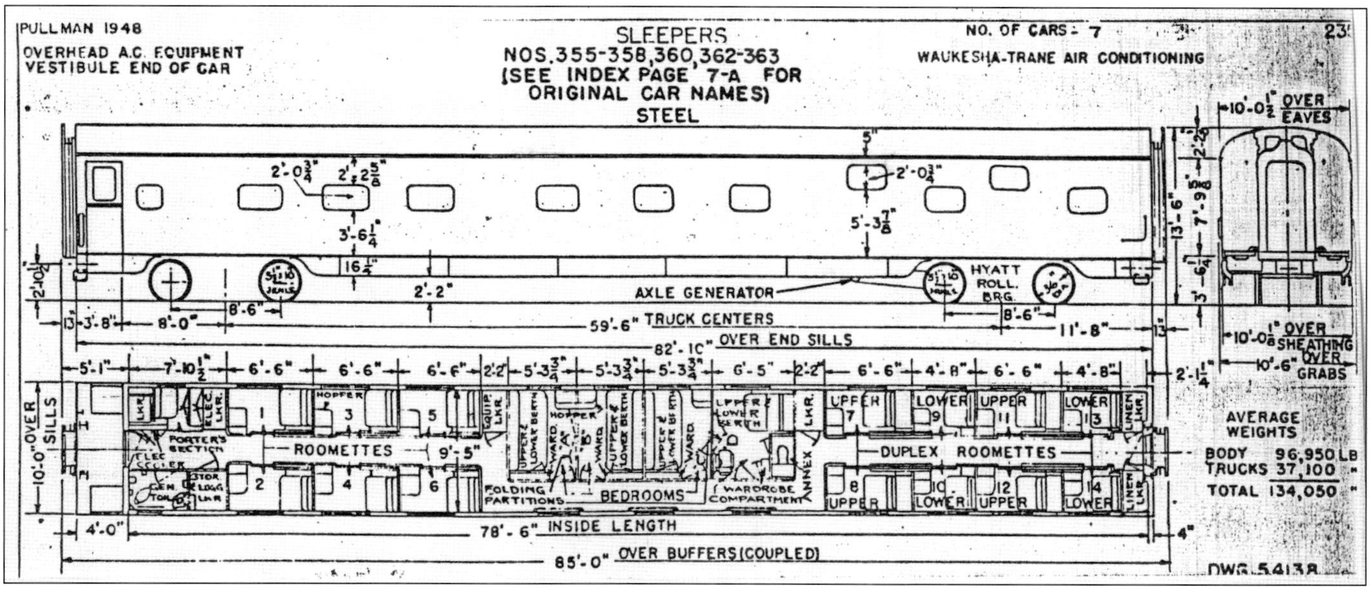

The Streamlined sleeping cars rode on four-wheel trucks, and had new types of rooms. This Northern Pacific sleeping car was equipped with 8 duplex roomettes, 6 roomettes, 3 double bedrooms and 1 compartment. *NP Diagram, Author's Collection*

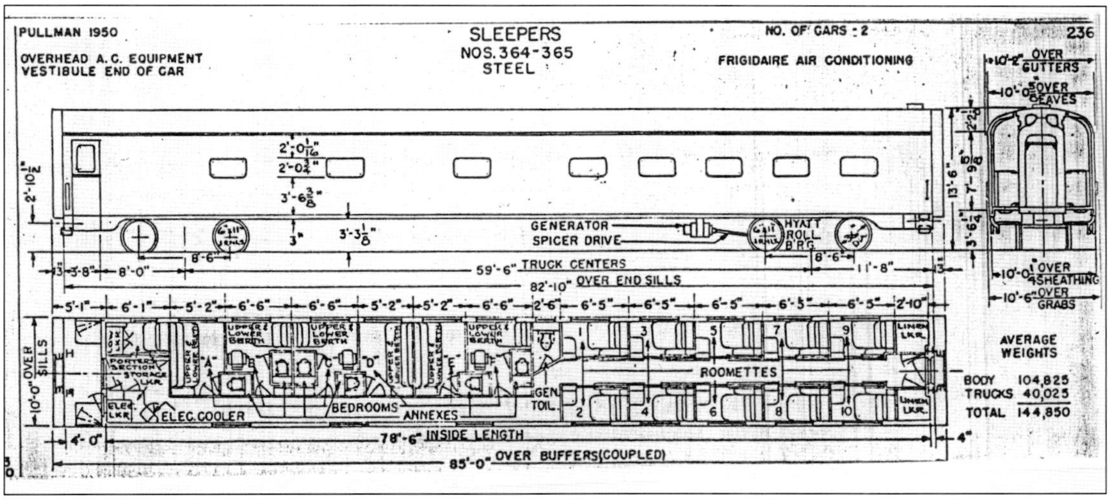

One of the more common streamlined sleepers was the 10-roomette, 6 double bedroom cars as illustrated here. *NP Diagram, Author's Collection*

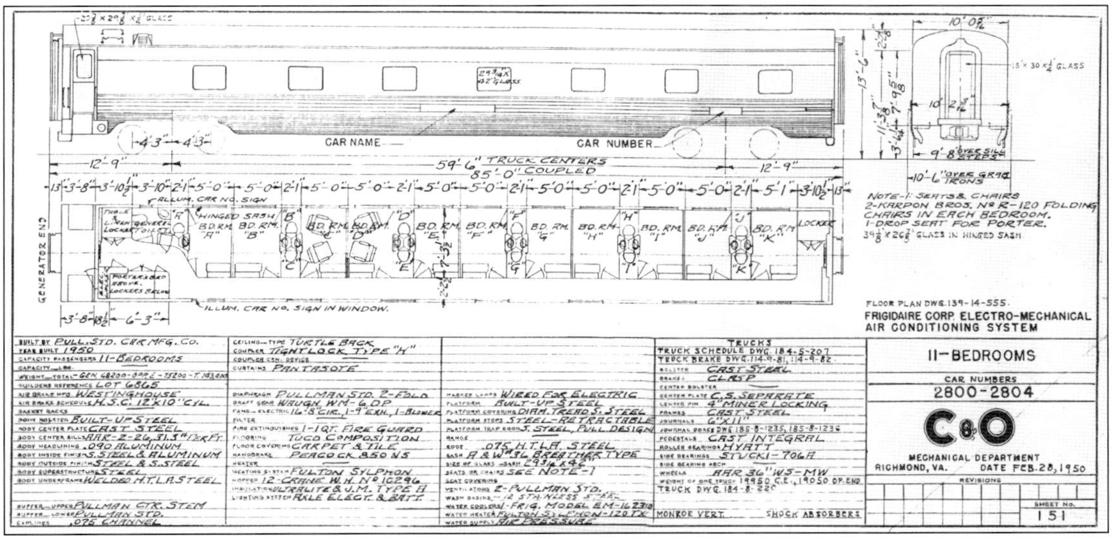

C&O sleeping cars in number series 2800 to 2804 were equipped with 11 double bedrooms and were 85 feet long. *C&O Diagram, Author's Collection*

Sleeping cars were commonly the last group within the consist of a passenger train. This photo of the Missouri-Kansas-Texas Railroad's Katy Flyer illustrates the last car, which is a Pullman 12-section, 1 drawing room car with a capacity for 27, one in each upper and lower berth and 3 in the drawing room. A dining car is ahead of the Pullman, two coaches ahead of the diner, and four head-end cars including one RPO-baggage just ahead of the first coach. Note that the entire train is basically in the Pullman Green color scheme, the common color for passenger equipment for decades. There were exceptions with the Pennsylvania Railroad using Tuscan Red, the Soo Line using Maroon, and two-tone gray schemes on the Union Pacific and Southern Pacific. This, of course, is not a complete list of color schemes for the North American railroads. The Katy Flyer is shown here at Oswego, Missouri, on June 14, 1942. *William Raia*

Heavyweight Pullman sleeper Glen Athol is a 6-compartment, 3 double bedroom car with a capacity for 18 people. Although, more could fit in with the various bed sizes. The car is in the two-tone grey scheme commonly found on the New York Central. In this case, the car is in the consist of a Milwaukee Road train at Milwaukee, Wisconsin. *Jim Scribbins, William Raia Collection*

Pullman sleeper Schubert illustrates the opposite side of the 6-compartment, 3 double bedroom car as compared to the photo of the Glen Athol. This photo shows the hallway side of the car in Chicago, April 27, 1967. *William Raia*

Pullman Oak Shade is a 12 roomette, 1 single bedroom, 4 double bedroom car in the two-tone gray color scheme. This is a rebuilt car, and this type was often part of the Soo Line's Laker between Chicago and Duluth, although in Southern Pacific two-tone gray color schemes, photographed in Milwaukee, July 6, 1965. *Jim Scribbins, William Raia Collection*

This photo shows a Walther's HO gauge heavyweight Pullman in the Southern Pacific's two-tone gray colors. When the railroad name was in the letter board, the Pullman name was in sub-lettering generally in the upper corners of both ends of the car as can be observed in this photo. *Dan Mackey*

The word "section" for the description of sleeping car accommodations meant upper and lower berths, which could be made up from the style of seating illustrated here. The two seats below pulled together to form the lower berth, while the upper berth was lowered from above. Note the curved base of the upper berths above the lower berth lamps. *Milwaukee Road Photo from 1927, Patrick C. Dorin Collection*

Burlington's Pullman "Silver Ravine" was a 10 roomette, 6 double bedroom car with seating for 22 passengers. Four roomettes were located at the vestibule end (two on each side), while the six double bedrooms were located in the middle. The final 6 roomettes were located at the left end of the car in this view. Note the sub-lettering Pullman in the upper corners at each end. *Owen Leander, William Raia Collection*

Burlington's Silver Swan, a 6 double bedroom, 5 compartment car, was in Amtrak service when this photo was taken in Chicago on October 31, 1971. Although the Pullman Company was no longer involved with sleeping car operations, the Burlington cars still carried the sub-lettering. *Owen Leander, William Raia Collection*

C&O's Old Point Comfort, #2605, was a 10 roomette, 6 double bedroom car. The car was still in service for the C&O and the B&O when its portrait was taken in Chicago in March 1969. *Owen Leander, William Raia Collection*

Canadian Pacific's Chateau Radisson was an 8 duplex roomette, 1 drawing room, 2 double bedroom and 4 section car. The car is shown here in the consist of the Canadian at Calgary, Alberta, in November 1967. *William Raia*

CP's 4 roomette, 5 double bedroom, 1 compartment, 4 section sleeper was part of the Manor series. The Douglas Manor is shown here at Calgary, Alberta, in December 1966. The letter board for the CP's corrugated side equipment was painted in the CP Tuscan Red colors with gold lettering. *William Raia*

Great Northern's Stevens Pass was an 8 duplex roomette, 4 double bedroom, 4 section sleeping car. The car operated on the Empire Builder with the name of train in the letter board. *Pullman Standard, John Sward Collection*

GN's Harrison Glacier was a 16 duplex roomette, 4 double bedroom sleeping car, built for operation on the Empire Builder. *Pullman Standard, John Sward Collection*

Amtrak sleeper #2420 was the only one of its kind on the roster in 1979. The car contained 8 duplex roomettes, 6 roomettes, and 4 double bedrooms. It was a former Northern Pacific Pullman sleeper, #372. In this picture it is part of the consist of the Empire Builder departing Minneapolis in October 1977. *Patrick C. Dorin*

Still another Northern Pacific car to go to Amtrak was the "slumbercoach," such as the Loch Sloy. Amtrak assigned slumbercoaches to the Empire Builder in the early 1970s, which operated with a variety of color schemes including the BN Cascade Green, the GN's Big Sky Blue and the Orange and Pullman Green, and even many other railroads, such as the Union Pacific sleeper just to the left of the NP slumbercoach. This photo was taken in June 1972 at LaCrosse, Wisconsin, on the Milwaukee Road. Amtrak operated the Empire Builder over the Milwaukee Road between Chicago and the Twin Cities. The NP and the Burlington Route slumbercoaches were built by the Budd Company. *Thomas Dorin*

The New York Central called their slumbercoaches "sleepercoaches." In addition to cars purchased directly from the Budd Company, the NYC rebuilt a few cars into a new version equipped with 16 roomettes and 10 double rooms. Sleepercoach #10810 was part of the NYC's 10810 to 10819 series. It is shown here at Springfield, Massachusetts, on January 1, 1966. *William Raia*

The Pullman Company created brochures illustrating the different types of sleeping car designs and accommodations such as the section, roomette, duplex roomette, double bedrooms, compartments, drawing room and lounge car facilities. *Author's Collection*

Here is one example of a bedroom in the streamlined cars. This photo shows the interior of a Pullman bedroom with an annex to the left with complete washroom facilities. The lower berth folded down from the wall behind the seat, while the upper berth was lowered from the ceiling. In addition to the sofa seat, a moveable chair was also part of the accommodations in the room. *Amtrak*

Chapter 8
DOME CARS

"Look up, look down and all around," is what passengers could do while riding in the dome cars operated on a number of western railroads. There were two basic types of domes. One was the short dome located in the center of the car. The other was a dome that extended for the entire length of the cars.

Dome cars were built with several designs. The most prominent was the dome coach, which was operated by the Baltimore and Ohio, the Union Pacific, the Burlington Route including the California Zephyr, the Great Northern, the Northern Pacific, and the Canadian Pacific.

Dome lounge cars were primarily the long dome type of cars, which operated on the Santa Fe, Great Northern, the Milwaukee Road and the Southern Pacific. However, there were the short dome designs for lounge cars on the Santa Fe and the Union Pacific, and dome observation cars on the Burlington.

Dome dining cars operated exclusively on the Union Pacific. However, the Canadian Pacific also operated a combination dome coffee shop and coach car on the Canadian.

Dome sleeping cars were operated on the Baltimore and Ohio's Capital Limited. The Northern Pacific also had dome sleeping cars for the North Coast Limited.

Dome cars were definitely a drawing card for passengers. It was great way to view the scenery. The Alaska Railroad still has dome cars for their train services.

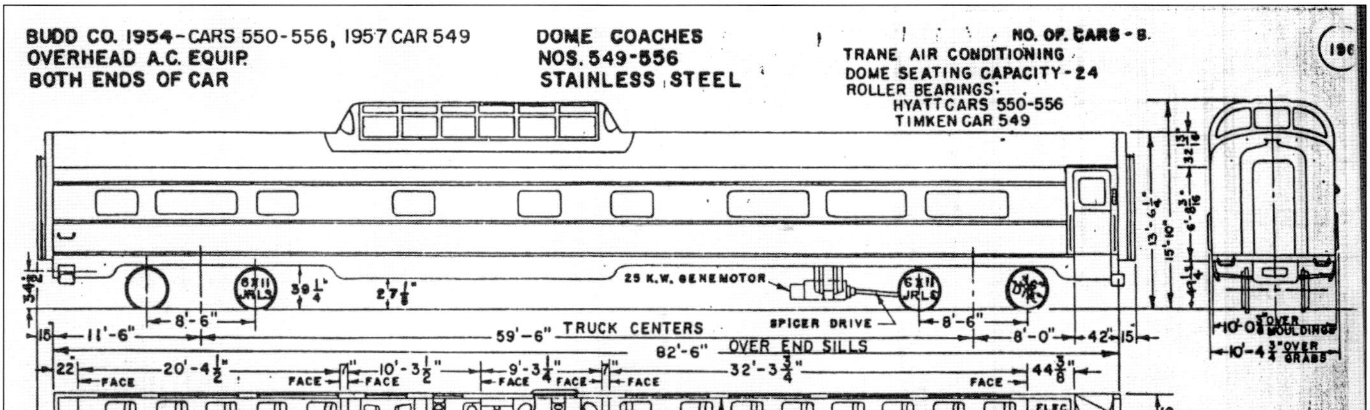

Dome coaches was a neat way to travel—and we can say they should be brought back. This Northern Pacific dome coach was assigned to the North Coast Limited, and provided leg-rest seating for 46 passengers. The dome was on the upper level as can be observed, while the washrooms were below the dome section. *NP Diagram, Author's Collection*

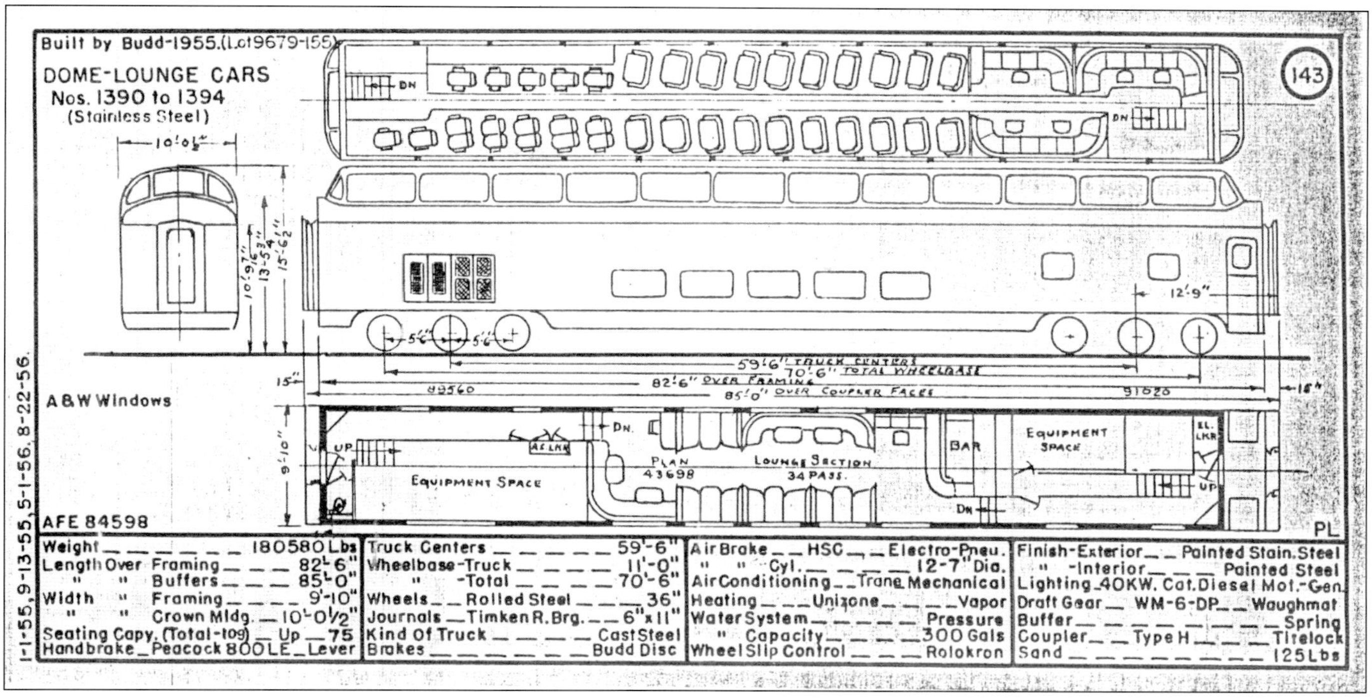

The Great Northern, the Santa Fe and the Milwaukee Road owned and operated full length dome lounge cars. *Great Northern Diagram, Author's Collection*

Burlington's dome coach Silver Vision, #4730 (4723 to 4730), provided seating for 54 passengers, and was operated on the Twin Cities Zephyrs as well as other Zephyrs. The car is shown here at Minneapolis in July 1971. *Owen Leander, William Raia Collection*

The California Zephyr operated over the Burlington, the Rio Grande and the Western Pacific between Chicago and the San Francisco Bay area. The Silver Lariat had a seating capacity of 46 seats. Leg-rest seating was provided in all of the dome coaches operated on the CZ. The CZ cars carried the train name in the letter board, while the railroad ownership was shown with the company reporting marks in the upper corners. Note the CB&Q for the Silver Lariat. *Owen Leander, William Raia*

Wabash dome parlor, #1602, was part of Blue Bird consist between Chicago and St. Louis. While the other Wabash cars had been built by the Budd Company with corrugated sides, the 1602 was built by Pullman Standard in 1952 with smooth sides. The car contained the "Blue Bird Room," a drawing room that accommodated up to 9 passengers. It may have been the largest drawing room to be operated on any railroad. *Originally Wabash Railroad, Patrick C. Dorin Collection*

Burlington Northern's dome coach #555 was the former Northern Pacific #555. The car originally operated on the North Coast Limited. This car, and a number of other former Great Northern and Northern Pacific cars, were assigned to operate on the Empire Builder and the North Coast Limited during the summer of 1971 when Amtrak went into service. *Patrick C. Dorin*

The Great Dome Lounge #1395, named the River View, was built for the Empire Builder and was owned by the Burlington. Note the CB&Q sub-lettering in the upper corners. Passenger equipment on the Empire Builder was painted in the GN colors, although part of the equipment was also owned by the Burlington and the Spokane, Portland and Seattle. The Great Dome Lounge provided snacks and beverages. *Owen Leander, William Raia Collection*

The Canadian Pacific finished the consist of the Canadian with a dome sleeper observation lounge car. The Assiniboine Park (part of the Park Series) contained 1 drawing room, 3 double bedrooms and the lounge area, photographed here in Calagary, Alberta, October 1966. *William Raia Collection*

Dome observation parlor cars were part of the Zephyr consists on the Burlington, such as the Twin Cities Zephyrs. The Silver View, #360, and #361, the Silver Vista, provided parlor car seating for 30 passengers. *Owen Leander, William Raia*

Great Northern dome coach #1325 (1320 to 1331) was eventually repainted in the Big Sky Blue scheme with white lettering. Seating capacity included 46 passengers in the coach seating (with leg-rests) and 24 in the dome. The GN operated the dome coaches in the Empire Builder, but they could also be part of the consist of the Western Star. Coach #1325 is shown here at Chicago on April 11, 1970. *Owen Leander, William Raia Collection*

Illinois Central dome coach #2211 (2210 to 2212) was originally a Missouri Pacific car. The car may have been in Amtrak service for a period of time as it is shown here at Chicago on August 29, 1971. *Owen Leander, William Raia Collection*

The Norfolk and Western, through its merger with the Wabash, acquired several dome coaches. Originally part of the Wabash "Blue Bird" between Chicago and St. Louis, #1612 (1610 to 1612) had seating capacity of 56 for the passengers, and 24 in the dome. *William Raia*

UPPER LEVEL

LOWER LEVEL

These photos are an example of an interior of a dome lounge car eventually operated by Amtrak. The tables at both levels indicate that the car was also used for furnishing snacks and light meals. Amtrak referred to the car as the "Discodome," as a rolling cabaret car, and operated on the Prairie State between Milwaukee, Chicago and St. Louis. *Amtrak Photo*

During the summer of 1971, Amtrak leased Sante Fe's big dome lounge car, #512 (506 to 513) for service on the Texas Chief. The seating capacity for this group of dome cars was 103 passengers. The cars were later sold to Auto-Train for their train service between Washington, D. C. and Sanford, Florida. The car is shown here departing the Union Station in Chicago in the Texas Chief, the name of which was eventually changed to the Lone Star. *Patrick C. Dorin*

Amtrak's dome lounge car #9373 was the former Southern Pacific's 3/4 length dome lounge #3604 from the number series 3600 to 3606. The cars had a variable seating capacities as follows: 3600 – 64 seats, 3601 to 3604 – 78 seats, and 3605 and 3606 – 74 seats. This photo was taken at the Great Northern Station in downtown Minneapolis in the early 1970s before the new Midway Station was built between Minneapolis and St. Paul. *Patrick C. Dorin*

This view shows the interior of the former Southern Pacific dome lounge cars with the different types of seating. *Amtrak*

Chapter 9
CAFÉ-COACHES and MORE

One very interesting concept with passenger car designs was, and is, the food and beverage services combined with coach seating or sleeping car accommodations. The concept has been utilized for well over a century and continues as we move through the first decade of the 21st Century.

The combination of coach seating with food and beverage services included such names as: diner-coach, dining lounge-coach, café-coach, coach lounge car, café lounge coach, coffee shop-coach, and there are many more names. In fact, one title as we move in the 21st Century is that of a dinette-coach. This combination concept has many benefits with the fact that food and beverage service can be provided with smaller trains, where a full dining car or diner-lounge car would be excessive. Combinations with coach seating are not the only configurations or car designs with this concept.

Sleeping cars are also part of the picture. During the days of the heavyweight standard equipment, there were many overnight trains that operated with a sleeper-dining lounge car. One example was the 8 section, restaurant lounge car. The car contained 8 sections providing upper and lower berth accommodations, a small kitchen in the car center, and table seating for up to 16 people (four tables with four seats at each table) and lounge car seating.

One example of a streamlined car was the 8 duplex roomette, 2 double bedroom, buffet lounge car, which was operated by the Great Northern on the Winnipeg Limited between St. Paul and Winnipeg. There were many other combinations with sleeping accommodations, such as sleeper observation lounge cars. This was also true with the standard heavyweight cars. An entire book could be written about the combinations of sleeping car accommodations with food and beverage services. Many of the railroads had their own specific designs reflecting the company's philosophy, and often used a variety of names, such as buffet lounge.

Food and beverage service facilities were also combined with parlor car seating. This included not only diner-parlor cars, but also such variations as parlor observation lounge or parlor buffet lounge. Although parlor car seating required first class ticketing, coach passengers were able to use the food and beverage services.

It should be mentioned that the combination food and beverage services was not limited to coaches, parlor cars or sleeping cars. A very interesting concept was the combination of food and beverage services with baggage cars. There were many concepts with this particular type, such as baggage tavern lounge cars, baggage tap café lounge cars, or simply baggage lounge cars.

There were still other concepts involving the combination of food and beverage facilities, such as dormitory lounge cars or dormitory coffee shop lounge cars. Such combinations of equipment were operated with overnight or transcontinental train services.

The combination food and beverage services with other types of equipment provided some interesting alternatives for passenger operations. For shorter trains, the combination equipment would provide adequate seating and access for meals and beverages for the smaller passenger loads. On the other hand, trains with larger passenger loads, such as transcontinental trains and many overnight services, such as New York Central's 20th Century Limited, the equipment provided additional facilities without overdoing the need for food and beverage services.

This type of equipment also provided drawing cards for repeat passengers. Just one example was the baggage tap café lounge cars operated on the Flambeau 400 between Chicago and Ashland, Wisconsin. The train was quite long between Chicago and Green Bay and it included a full dining car. The size of the train was reduced to five cars between Green Bay and Ashland, which included an RPO-baggage car, the baggage tap café lounge car, two coaches and one parlor car. The combination baggage tap café lounge provided the food and beverage services for the 250 miles north of Green Bay.

There is no doubt about it, the combination of food and beverage facilities with passenger accommodations did much for the enhancement of rail passenger services.

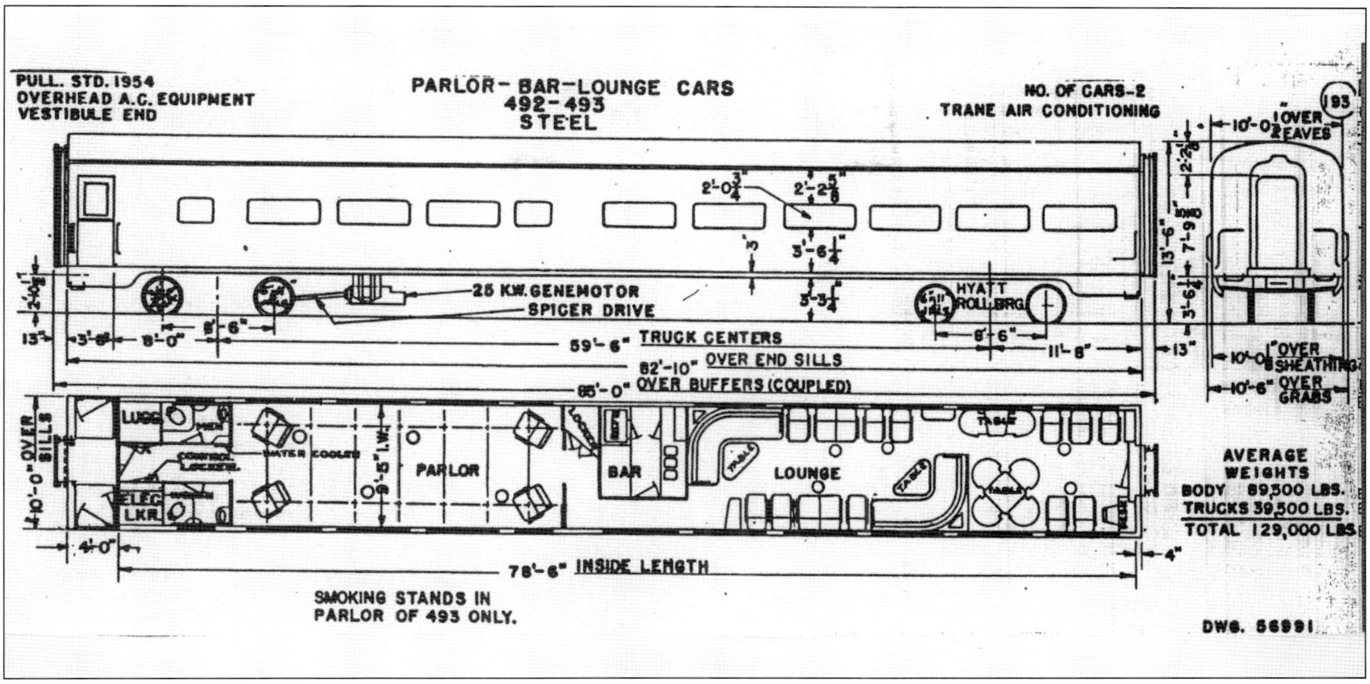

There were many designs for combining revenue seating with food and beverage facilities. This parlor bar lounge was operated by the Northern Pacific and provided parlor car seating and beverage services. *NP Diagram, Author's Collection*

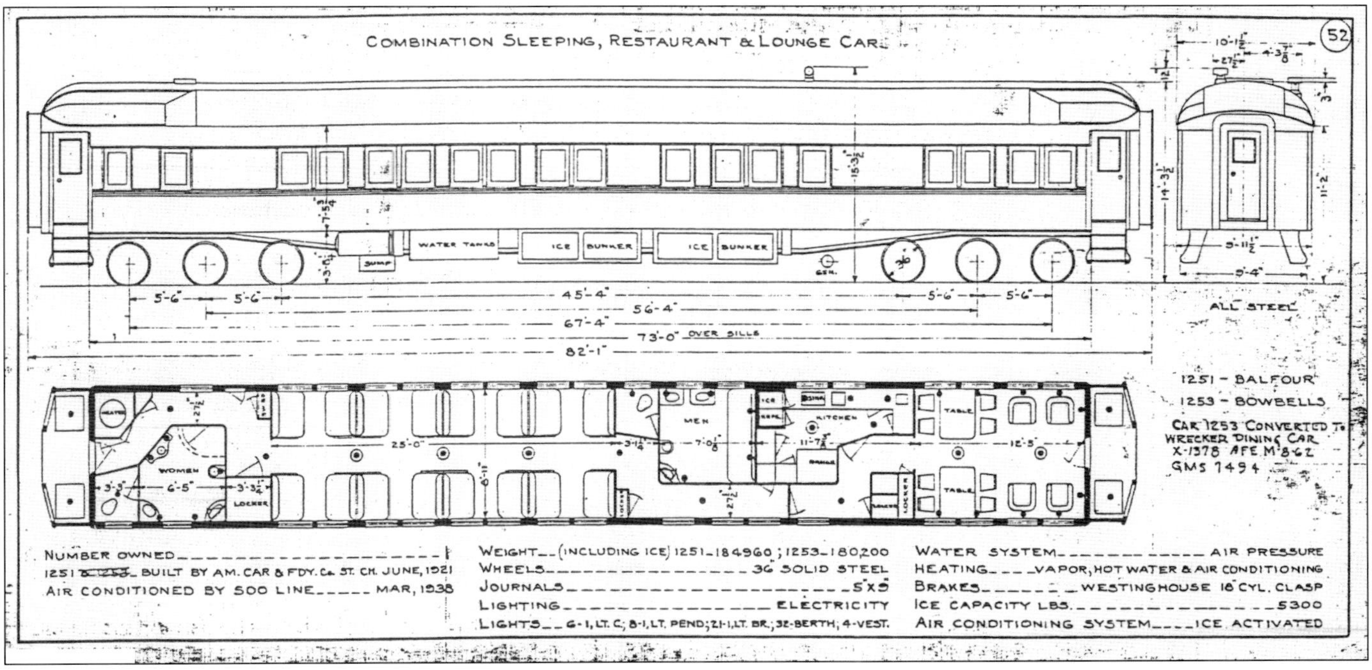

The Soo Line's sleeping, restaurant-lounge car is one example of the heavyweight designs operated by the railroads. *Soo Line Diagram, Author's Collection*

This Great Northern café-parlor car was downgraded for work train service. It was a rebuilt car with a streamlined roof with the number series 1060 and 1061. Such equipment operated on a variety of trains on the Great Northern. *Patrick C. Dorin*

Erie-Lackawanna diner parlor #751 was 79 feet, 2 inches long, and provided seating for 18 passengers in the parlor section, and 16 in the dining room. The photo was taken at Hoboken, New Jersey, in June 1969. *Harold K. Vollrath Collection*

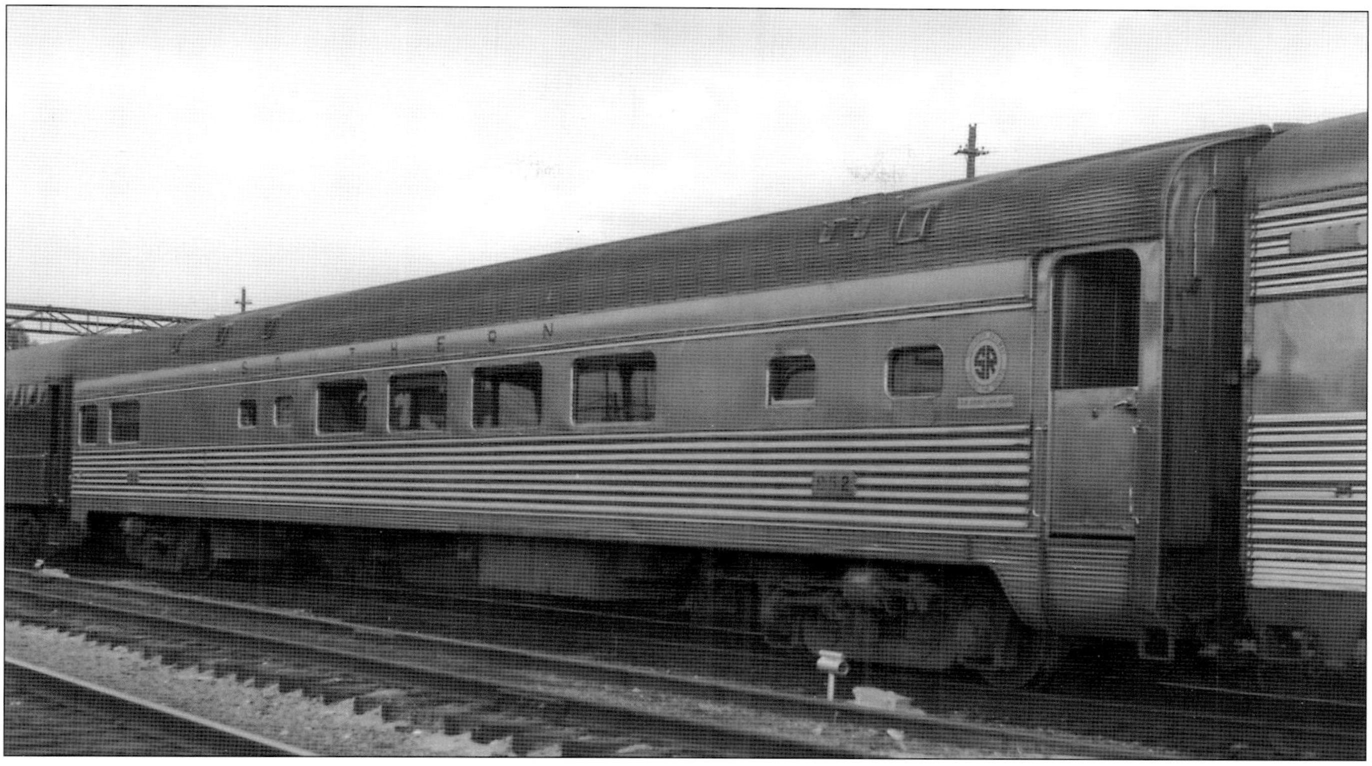

Southern Railway lounge coach #952 (950 to 955) provided seating for 46 passengers. The car is shown here at Salisbury, North Carolina, in May 1955. *Harold K. Vollrath Collection*

Norfolk County is a combination sleeper lounge car, a 10 section lounge. The car is shown here at Cincinnati, Ohio, in May 1967. *F. Hirsch, William Raia Collection*

The Pullman Dover Fort is a 6 double bedroom, buffet lounge car. Note the two-tone gray color scheme. *F. Hirsch, William Raia Collection*

This Pennsylvania car is a coach bar lounge car, #1152 (1151), and had seating for 40 passengers. The car is at Louisville, Kentucky, on May 15, 1964. *Jim Scribbins, William Raia Collection*

This Illinois Central car is a combination food bar coach. It is equipped with a radio antenna on the roof, and is shown here at Chicago on May 20, 1972. Quite likely it is in Amtrak service. The number of the car is not visible. Note the six-wheel trucks on this very attractive piece of equipment. *Owen Leander, William Raia Collection*

The New Haven Railroad's Bay State is a combination 6 double bedroom, buffet lounge car. The double bedrooms are to the right, while the lounge area is to the left. Photographed in South Boston, on August 17, 1968. *William Raia*

Southern Railway coach lounge #950 (950 to 955 Series) is shown here at Lexington, Kentucky, on April 12, 1969. *Jim Scribbins, William Raia Collection*

The Seaboard's Sun Beam was a 5 double bedroom, buffet lounge car. The car was originally named the Palm Beach and was renamed in 1967. This equipment had a very pleasant window arrangement for the lounge area, which is to the right in this photo. Note the overhead wire for the electric power for the Pennsylvania Railroad. When this photo was taken in New York on September 17, 1970, the Seaboard Railroad had merged with the Atlantic Coast Line. The new railroad name was the Seaboard Coast Line, which is now part of CSX. *William Raia*

Chapter 10
OBSERVATION CARS

The observation car was, and is, a very popular car for passengers. They had a chance to sit and view the passing scenery and look at the trackage to the rear as the train rolled along. Viewing out of the rear of the train provided an opportunity to see areas on both sides of the track.

The standard heavyweight cars had to two basic types of observation cars. One was the open-end car, while the other was an enclosed observation room with larger windows. The streamliner cars had enclosed ends but were either squared off or rounded. Often the squared end cars had a diaphragm at the rear door, which permitted the cars to be operated in mid-train if necessary.

Observation cars were either full lounge or café lounge cars, or a combination with either sleeping accommodations or parlor car seating. These types of designs held true for both the heavyweights and the streamlined cars.

The heavyweight observation car design was also used for business cars, which are covered in Chapter 12. The observation cars were definitely a neat final car for any passenger train. With the potential for viewing from the rear of the train, and the artistic look that the cars provided for the passenger train consists, it added new levels of value for train travel. The cars served in many ways as an invitation for the traveling public to take the train.

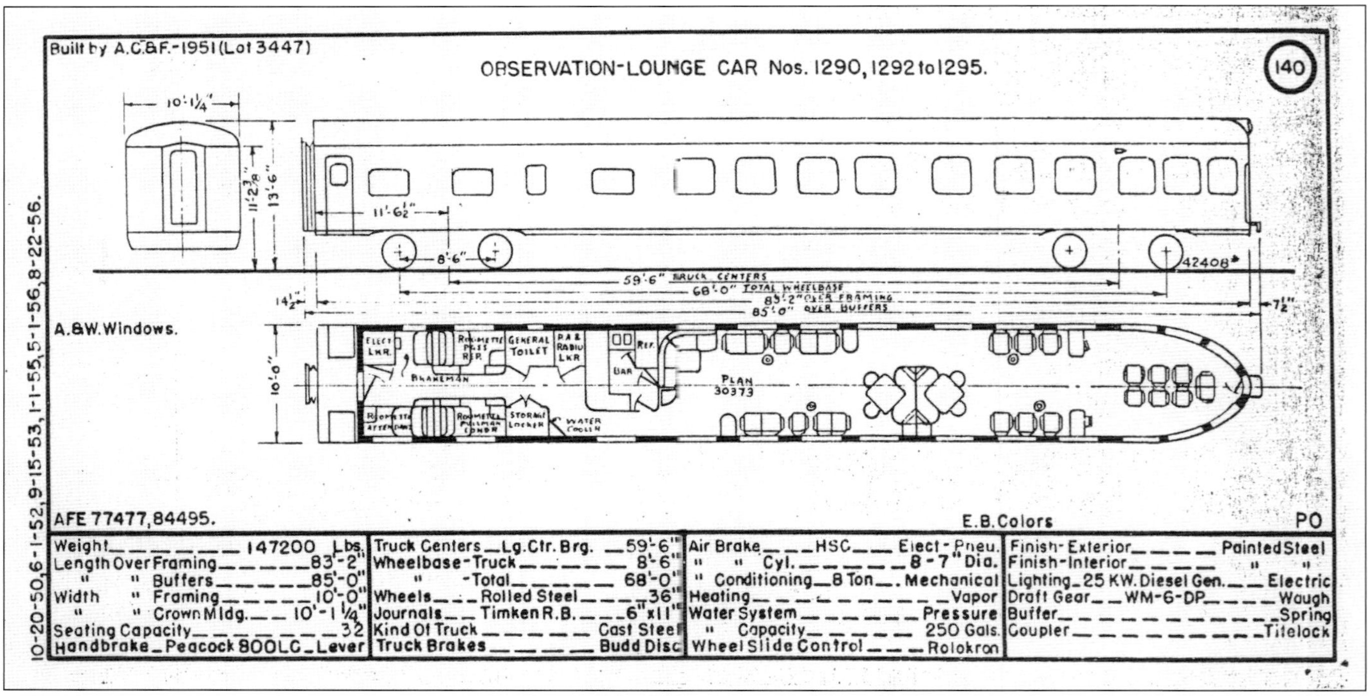

There were two basic types of observation cars. The heavyweight cars were generally open-end, although some were constructed with squared ends without the open platform. Streamlined cars had either round ends, as can be observed with this diagram, or with squared ends. Observation cars were generally the last car of a consist. *Great Northern Diagram, Author's Collection*

New York Central's Huron River was a parlor observation car that operated on the Twilight Limited. The car had a seating capacity of 31 passengers. *William Raia*

Pennsylvania Railroad's Detroit Arrow included the parlor observation car, the Queen Mary. This car was very similar to the New York Central's Huron River. Note the word "Pullman" in the letter board. The photo was taken at Detroit in 1939. *Harold K. Vollrath Collection*

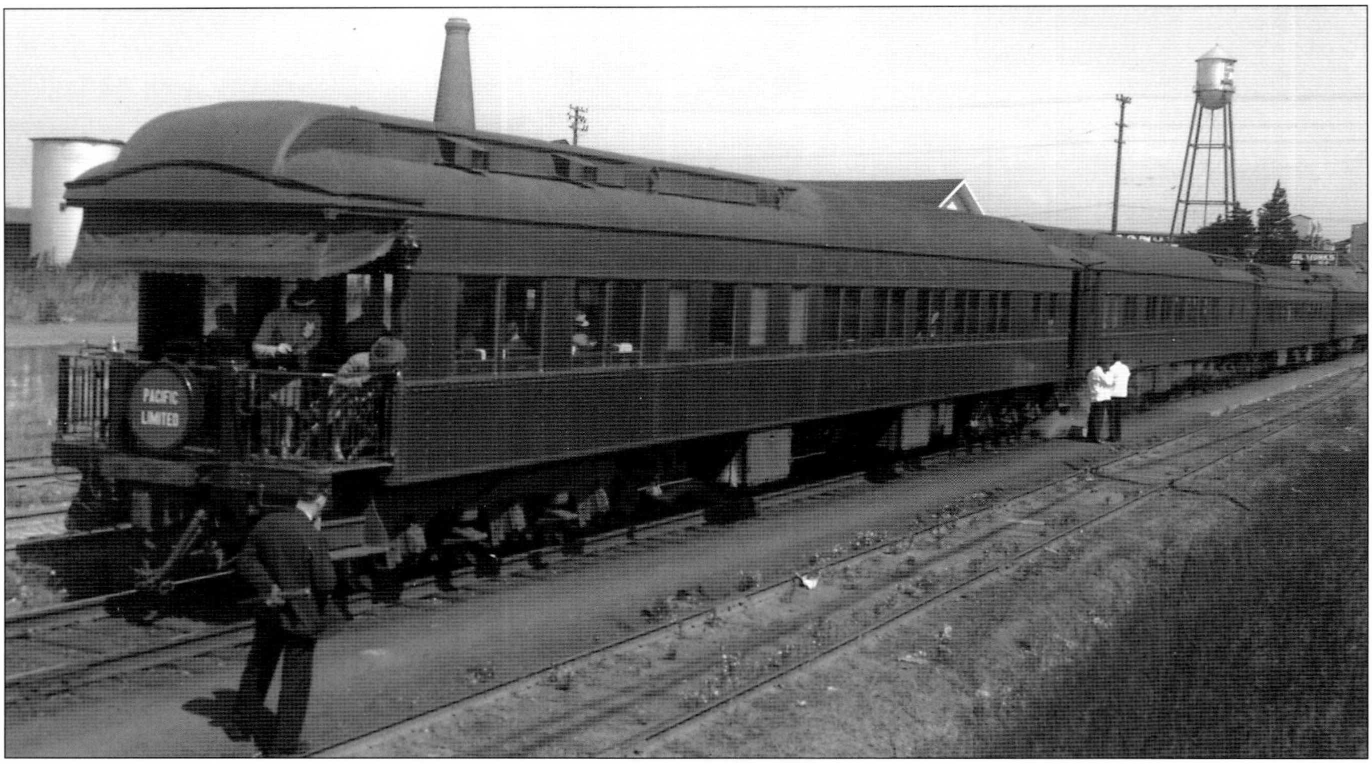

Another example of Heavyweight Observation Cars was the Southern Pacific's Mt. Marcy, a 10 section observation lounge car. It is shown here on the Pacific Limited in Berkeley, California, in August 1940. *Harold K. Vollrath Collection*

Pullman car Mt. Sheridan was a 10 section, observation lounge car, and is shown here on the rear of the Cotton Belt's train #201, the Lone Star at Shreveport, Louisiana, in May 1949. *Harold K. Vollrath Collection*

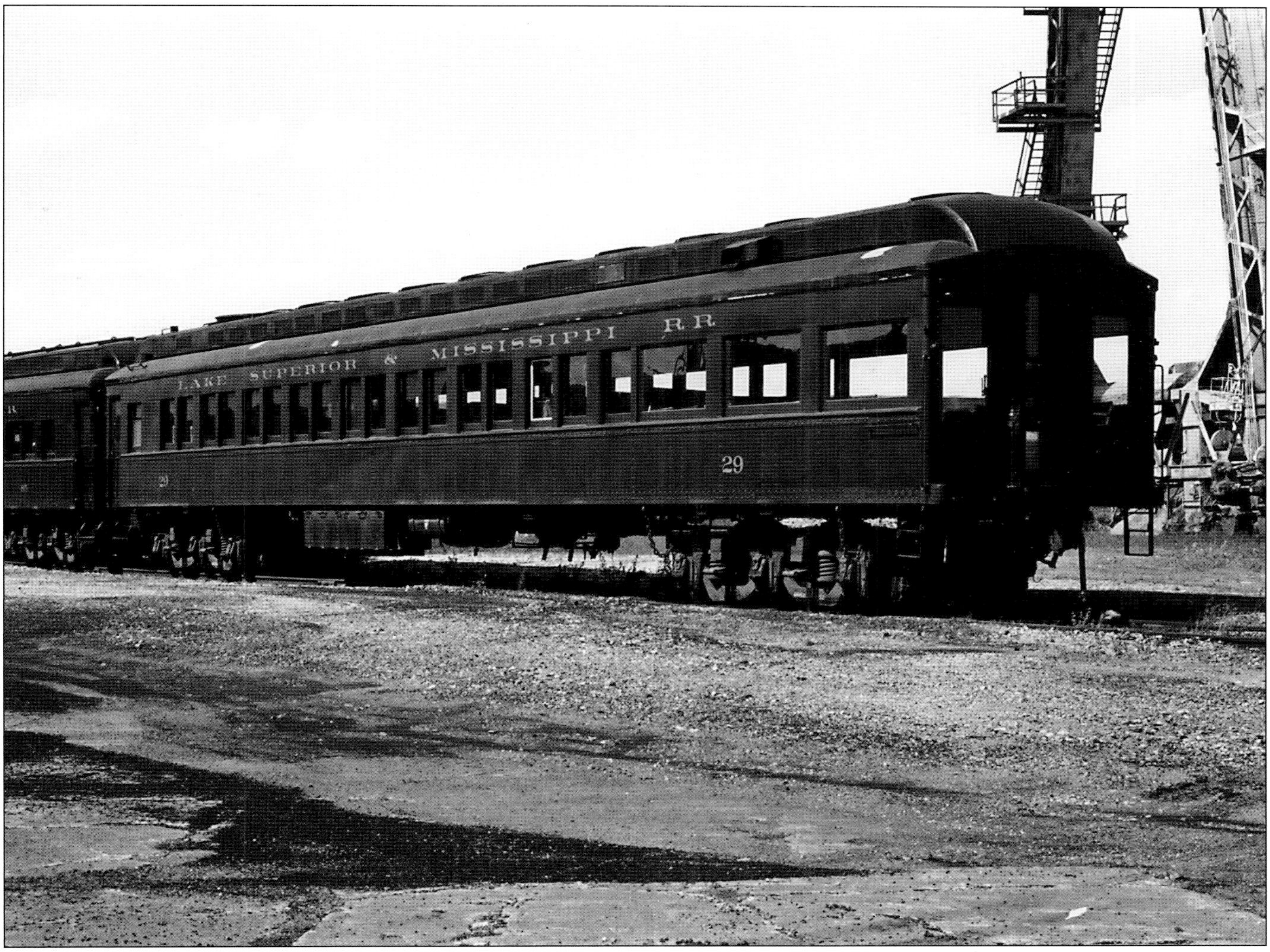

Here is an example of a heavyweight coach observation car without the open end platform. The Duluth, Missabe and Iron Range Railway operated two of these cars on trains between Duluth and Hibbing, and Duluth and Ely, Minnesota. The car is shown here re-lettered for the Lake Superior and Mississippi Railroad, a tourist line in West Duluth that follows the St. Louis River. *Patrick C. Dorin*

The Canadian National purchased the Milwaukee Road sky-top lounge sleeping cars after the discontinuance of the Olympian Hiawatha between Chicago and Seattle. The CN operated the cars on the Super Continental between Montreal and Vancouver. *Jim Scribbins*

Pennsylvania Railroad's Martha Washington brings up the rear of one of the fast Washington-New York trains at North Philadelphia in May 1951. The Martha Washington and the Benjamin Franklin were designated as parlor-bar-phone observation cars. *Harold K. Vollrath Collection*

The Florida East Coast Railroad also owned observation cars, such as the Bay Biscayne, shown here at Miami in 1944, and the Lake Worth. The cars were combination tavern observation lounge cars and were 85 feet long. *Harold K. Vollrath Collection*

This Baltimore and Ohio observation car is gracing the rear of the northbound Cincinnatian at Deshler, Ohio, in February 1955. *William S. Kuba*

Pennsylvania Railroad's Samuel Rea was a 1 double bedroom, 1 compartment, 2 drawing room, buffet lounge observation car. *William Raia*

The Pullman "Pepper Pike Country Club" is an 8 section, 1 compartment, restaurant observation lounge car. The car does not have the open platform, but rather windows at the end of the car for viewing the passing scenery. It would be interesting to know the precise owner/operator of the car since it does not have a rail name in the letter board. The photo was taken in Chicago in 1940. *J. Buckley, William Raia Collection*

Illinois Central parlor observation car #3827 is bringing up the rear of a special train at Freeport, Illinois, in 1940. The car is one of the older designs as one can tell by the types of windows. Often, the upper section of the windows were replaced by panels. The tail sign is difficult to read, but it appears to say "Baseball Game." *J. Buckley, William Raia Collection*

The Pullman "Mountain Road" is a 10 section, observation lounge car and is shown here at Chicago in December 1940. The car is in the common Pullman Green scheme with the gold lettering. *W. Ranke, William Raia Collection*

Chapter 11
THE POST 1970s ERA

Amtrak has been operation since 1971. VIA Rail Canada has been in operation since the 1970s. The Alaska Railroad still operates its own passenger trains without being part of the Amtrak System. Furthermore, there are many tourist railroads in operation throughout North America. Each of these railroad passenger systems still operate passenger equipment that was built during the 1940s into the 1960s, as well as operating new equipment that were based on the designs of streamlined passenger equipment in operation since the 1940s.

There have been many passenger cars that have gone through extensive rebuilding. This includes all types of equipment from head-end cars to observation cars. The purpose of this chapter is to review some of the passenger equipment from the 1940s through the 1960s and continued service even into the 21st Century, plus new equipment that is very similar. Just one example happens to be Amtrak's Superliners, upon which the basic idea was drawn (in a variety of ways) from the Hi-Level cars constructed for the Santa Fe's El Capitan.

New bi-level passenger equipment, operated by Amtrak California, has its design roots (with many modifications and changes to accommodate passengers in the 21st Century) in some of the bi-level cars constructed for both commuter service and the long distance C&NW bi-level 400 equipment.

The Alaska Railroad also operates rebuilt passenger equipment from the 1950s and 1960s that were purchased from such rail lines as the Union Pacific and Burlington Northern. The fleet includes dome coaches and dining cars as well as other equipment.

Furthermore, some of the newest equipment built in the 1990s (or later) is very much like the equipment purchased from railroads in the lower 48. This includes new coaches from South Korea as well as other types of equipment.

It just goes to demonstrate that the passenger car designs covering several decades have a lot of merit for providing high quality passenger service. Furthermore, it is interesting to note that many types of passenger equipment built during the 1940s (and later) were capable of operating at speeds up to 120 miles per hour. There is much to learn from our passenger car designs of many years ago. We cannot forget that!

Amtrak operated a small fleet of Rail Diesel Cars on some of their short distance trains, such as the Black Hawk shown here. The three RDC-1s provided unreserved coach seating as well as snack and refreshment service. The Black Hawk operated as trains 371 westbound and 370 eastbound between Chicago and Dubuque, Iowa, a distance of 182 miles. *William Raia*

Amtrak repainted many of the former individual railroad company passenger equipment, such as illustrated with the 10 roomette, 6 double bedroom car, the Pacific Crest, #2436. The car was built by the Budd Company, and refurbished by Amtrak after the 1971 start-up. *Patrick C. Dorin*

Amtrak coach #6805 was formerly a Great Northern observation car. The car was originally built in 1950 by Pullman Standard as a sleeper observation lounge car, #1197, the Grand Coulee. It was rebuilt again as a sleeper observation lounge, #1197, with the name Priest River. In 1968 it was rebuilt as a full coach for 68 passengers by the GN. The 6805 is shown here at Seattle in 1975. *Patrick C. Dorin*

Amtrak table car (dining room) #8602 was a former leg-rest coach. Amtrak placed the car in dining car service for the Auto-Train. *Patrick C. Dorin*

Amfleet coach designs were based on the original Pennsylvania Railroad Metroliners built by the Budd Company. *Patrick C. Dorin*

The view illustrates the interior of the Amfleet Coaches. *Patrick C. Dorin*

Burlington Route dome cars were a favorite for Amtrak on the various transcontinental services. Amtrak #9811, the Silver Lounge, is part of the consist of train #9, the North Coast Hiawatha, at Billings, Montana, in December 1976. The car was originally a Burlington Route dome buffet lounge dormitory car, #251. It was built by the Budd Company in 1948. *Patrick C. Dorin*

Amtrak dome coach #9410 was repainted after leaving the Burlington Northern service. *Patrick C. Dorin*

The Santa Fe Hi-level cars were also incorporated into the Amtrak system of passenger equipment. Amtrak #9984 is a Hi-level dining car, which was once Santa Fe's #654. The Hi-level cars were built by the Budd Company in 1956 with additional cars arriving in 1963 and 1964. The 9984 is part of the consist of the Southwest Limited at Winslow, Arizona, in May 1976. *A. Robert Johnson, Patrick C. Dorin Collection*

Amtrak repainted several of the C&NW bi-level 400 coaches, which were operated on such trains as the Chicago-Valparaiso, Indiana commuter service. The ex-400 Coaches were equipped with reclining seats, which made them different from the commuter bi-levels, even though in many ways the cars were identical with the exteriors. *Patrick C. Dorin*

Interior view of the upper gallery level of an ex-400 bi-level coach with single seating. *Patrick C. Dorin*

The lower level of the gallery cars were equipped with paired seating. This was the case for both commuter cars and long distance coaches on the C&NW as well as other railroads with gallery type bi-level equipment. *Patrick C. Dorin*

Metra bi-level cab coach #8740 was part of a fleet of bi-level commuter coaches built for the Chicago and North Western in 1959-60. The equipment lost its yellow and green colors and was eventually repainted in the Metra color scheme for the Chicago area commuter rail service. The 8740 is shown here at Elgin, Illinois, in March 1999. *Patrick C. Dorin*

This bi-level cab coach #8718 displays the Regional Transportation Authority (RTA) color scheme. RTA was the overseer of the commuter rail services on all of the Chicagoland railroads. Thus the equipment and motive power were originally painted in RTA colors, and later replaced by the Metra colors illustrated in the previous photo. This train is shown here at the Chicago and North Western Station in Chicago in July 1998. The colors are another example of equipment dating back to the 1950s and 1960s with repainting and in full service. *Patrick C. Dorin*

This Metra cab coach resembles the type of equipment built for the Burlington Route in 1950 by the Budd Company. The design was, and is, considered very good and has led to the purchase of additional equipment for the last fifty-some years. *Patrick C. Dorin*

The bi-level design led to the development of bi-level electric multiple unit equipment, which was placed in operation on the Illinois Central during the 1970s. The new name for the IC service is Metra Electric, and this illustration shows the similarity of the bi-level designs with the commuter equipment operated by Metra. *Patrick C. Dorin*

For a brief period of time during the late 1990s, Amtrak operated a commuter train service between Milwaukee and Watertown, Wisconsin. The equipment selected for the service was the new Horizon Coaches, which were developed in the 1980s. The cars are similar to the coaches in operation ever since the streamliner design took place. The only difference is that the cars are not quite as tall as the standard streamlined cars—approximately a foot shorter. The commuter train is shown here at Watertown in June 1998. *Patrick C. Dorin*

Amtrak purchased a fleet of equipment based on the designs of the Hi-level cars for the Santa Fe. The equipment included coaches, lounge cars, dining cars, sleeping cars, and even combination coaches with a baggage area at the lower level. The cars operated on the transcontinental trains, as well as on some of the eastern routes to Washington, D.C. There were other cases where the equipment has operated on shorter distance trains. This train happens to be a North Star en route from Minneapolis to Duluth, Minnesota at Saunders, just to the south of Superior, Wisconsin. *Patrick C. Dorin*

The new Superliner equipment with the Hi-level concept included new designs for sleeping car services, such as the #32003. The cars provide roomettes (or sometimes called economy rooms) as well as bedrooms and a family room. *Patrick C. Dorin*

The interiors of dining cars as we move into the 21st Century is very similar to the table seating in diners or café cars dating back to the late 19th Century. Table seating is still one of the most convenient ways to enjoy a meal at any time of the day. *Patrick C. Dorin*

Amtrak dining car #8510 is shown here as part of the consist of the North Star at Duluth, Minnesota, in July 1980. The North Star provided overnight train service between Duluth and Chicago via Minneapolis and St. Paul. *Patrick C. Dorin*

The dome lounge car, #9301, the Mountain View, was the former Great Northern car #1392. *Patrick C. Dorin*

Auto-Train launched a new train service in the United States between Washington, D.C. and Sanford, Florida. It was later transferred to Amtrak. Auto carrier #9029 is a bi-level car. Amtrak also operates tri-level auto carriers. *Patrick C. Dorin*

The original Auto-Train, before it became part of Amtrak, had its own complete lettering. Car #598 was a buffet-entertainment car. The cars served cafeteria style meals and showed movies after the meal periods. This particular car was originally owned by the Atlantic Coast Line and later by the Chesapeake and Ohio. *Patrick C. Dorin*

The Northern Indiana Commuter Transportation District operates the South Shore commuter route between Chicago, Gary, Michigan City and South Bend, Indiana. During the early 1980s, the South Shore purchased a fleet of new single level, electric MU coaches for the commuter train service. This train is arriving at Dune Park, Indiana, en route to Chicago from South Bend during the late fall of 1988. *Patrick C. Dorin*

Interior Coach seating on the South Shore streamlined MU is quite comfortable. The design is more relaxing than the former flip-over seats that were once common on commuter cars. *Patrick C. Dorin*

The Northern Indiana Commuter Transportation District ordered new electric multiple unit bi-level coaches with delivery taking place in 2009. The basic design is similar to the bi-level approach which has been in operation since the 1950s in the Chicago area. Note the placement of the cab at the end of the bi-level coach. *NICTD*

The newest passenger equipment to arrive in the U.S. as of the summer of 2009 are the new bi-level commuter coaches built by Bombardier for the new commuter service between Minneapolis and Big Lake. The coaches are the same basic design that have been in operation on GO Transit, the commuter train service for the Toronto, Ontario area. The first such equipment went into operation during the 1970s. This photo illustrates the new North Star commuter train equipment, Coach No. 708. This is one of the newest commuter train services to be launched in North America as of this writing in late 2009. *David Bruns & Patrick C. Dorin*

Alaska Railroad dome coach #522 was obtained from the Burlington Northern. The Alaska Railroad acquired a substantial amount of passenger equipment from several railroads, such as the Great Northern, New Haven, Union Pacific, Southern Pacific, the Chicago and North Western and more. Much of the equipment had been built during the period from the late 1940s to even the early 1960s, and has been rebuilt for the Alaska Railroad passenger services. *Patrick C. Dorin*

Here are two photos of coaches (204 above, 210 below) built with a similar design from the 1940s to the 60s. The coaches, number series 205 to 210, were built in 1989 by Enprotech Corporation of New York, a subsidiary of C. Itoh of America, which is a Division of C. Itoh of Japan and Daewoo Heavy Industries of Korea.

The cars are painted in the dark blue and bright yellow. Each car contains 78 seats of which 74 recline. The cars are 85 feet long, 13 feet, 10 inches high and 10 feet wide. They are handicapped accessible. The coach windows (No. 210) are nearly 60 inches long and 36 inches high, designed to provide greater viewing. The coaches were photographed in Fairbanks in 2000. *Patrick C. Dorin*

Chapter 12
BUSINESS and INSPECTION CARS

Business and inspection cars have the same basic design as passenger equipment. There are a few exceptions, such as bi-level or double deck cars for business or inspection special trains.

Business cars are operated for inspection of the railroad lines, company meetings, and shipper specials. The interior accommodations include a crew room, kitchen, dining room, bedrooms, and observation lounge room. Business cars have been part of the passenger car rosters since the 1800s. The equipment included both the standard heavyweight as well as the streamlined lightweight designs.

Practically every railroad had some type of business car except for the smallest of the short lines or terminal railroads. Depending upon the policies of the individual railroad, part of the business car fleet could be assigned to specific managers or offices, such as the President, Vice President-Operations, Vice President-Traffic (Marketing), General Managers, and in some cases, Division Superintendents.

Business cars generally operated on the rear of a scheduled passenger train, or as part of special trains for shippers, safety meetings, track inspections or the Board of Directors. However, it was not uncommon to see a business car at the head-end of a passenger train or freight train, or on the rear of a freight train behind the caboose.

Business cars were rather unique cars, especially with the appearance of an open end observation car. Even the newer streamlined business cars had an open rear platform as had been the custom since such equipment was first built in 1800s.

Not all business cars were built as open end cars. Depending upon the use and operation of the car, they could have the appearance of a regular coach or a combination car. There were still other types of passenger equipment operated as part of the "special trains." These included sleeping cars, dining cars, instruction class cars, and even coaches and baggage cars. As we move through the 21st Century, baggage cars in special service are often equipped with head-end power to provide the electricity for the equipment lighting, heating and air-conditioning. This chapter also reviews some of the different types of business and inspection cars that have been in operation since the 1940s through the first decade of the 21st Century.

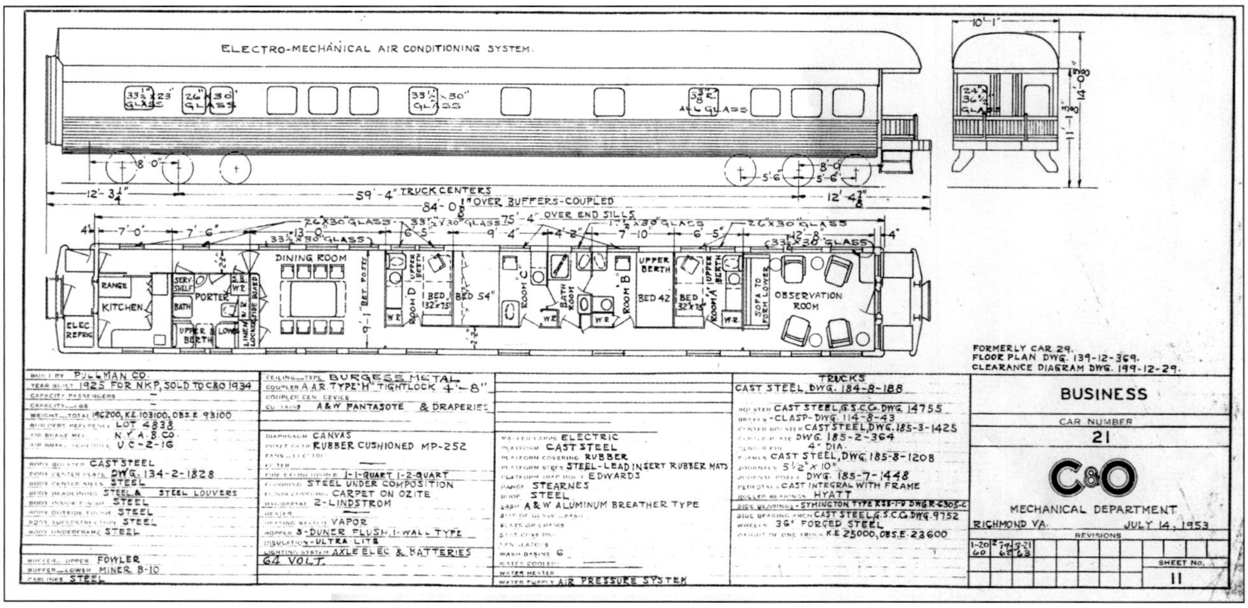

This C&O business car #21 is an example of a heavyweight car that has been rebuilt with fluted sides to match the new streamlined passenger equipment. Business cars generally had an open platform at the rear of the car for the observation room. *C&O Diagram, Author's Collection*

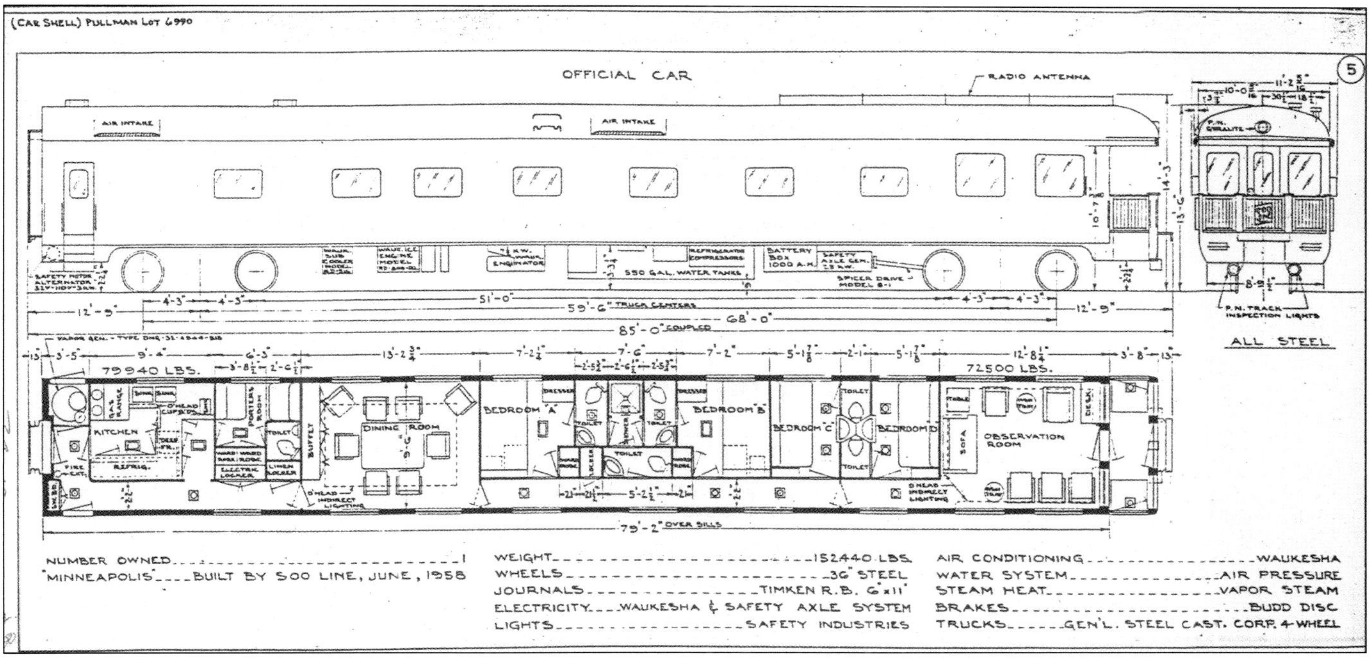

Soo Line business car, the Minneapolis, is a prime example of a streamlined car. Note that both diagrams illustrate how the kitchen and porter's room is at the front, the dining room is next, while the next section contains the bedrooms followed by the observation room. This equipment was excellent for inspection trips as well as presentations for potential freight customers. *Soo Line Diagram, Author's Collection*

Business cars also have a long history in the railroad industry. The Rio Grande #106, shown here at Bond, Colorado, in 1947, was built in 1889. The observation platform on the rear of the car was designed specifically for viewing and inspecting the railroad line. *Harold K. Vollrath Collection*

Business cars were normally on the rear end of a passenger or freight train, Normally the Business car would have the rear of the car facing back. In this case, we have two Baltimore and Ohio business cars with the open platforms connected together. The location of this B&O passenger train with four cars ahead of the business cars is unknown. *William S. Kuba Collection*

The Duluth, Missabe & Iron Range Railway business car, the Northland, served the railroad for inspection and business meeting trips for well over 50 years. The Northland is now assigned to Lake Superior Railroad Museum and is often operated on the North Shore Scenic Railroad (Duluth and Two Harbors, Minnesota) for special trips and parties. The Northland is shown here at the Duluth Union Station, now part of the Lake Superior Railroad Museum. *Patrick C. Dorin*

Santa Fe business car #39 (30 to 39) has been painted silver with simulated corrugated sides and letter board. The car ahead of the 39 is an inspection car with rear windows but without an open platform. *William Raia*

C&NW business car #100 (100 to 102) is a typical example of the heavyweight cars and painted in the Pullman Green colors with gold lettering on many railroads. The car was 82 feet, 1 inch long and is shown here at Chicago in July 1954. *F. Neider, William Raia Collection*

The Santa Fe streamlined business car with corrugated sides was #51 and carried the name "Topeka." It is shown here coupled to the rear of an Amtrak train operating over the Santa Fe. *William Raia*

Burlington Northern's business car, the Mississippi River, was a former Burlington car—note the corrugated sides and roof. The car ahead of the Mississippi River is the former GN parlor car that operated on the Great Northern. *Patrick C. Dorin*

Still another BN streamlined business car was the Yellowstone River, a former Northern Pacific car. It is shown here coupled to the rear of Amtrak's North Coast Hiawatha. *Patrick C. Dorin*

The Rio Grande's business car #100 is coupled to other passenger equipment at the Denver Station in July 1947. However, it can be said it is not yet on a train for departure since there are no marker lamps at the rear of the car. The picture windows at the rear of the car are designed specifically for the observation lounge area for business trips or inspection runs over the railroad. *William Raia*

The 90-mile Chicago, South Shore and South Bend Railroad (the Indiana commuter and freight rail route between Chicago and South Bend) owned a business car for meetings, business trips and inspection runs over the railroad. "Hiram" is shown here in August 1987, at Michigan City, Indiana, at the South Shore Shops facility. The car was painted in the orange and maroon scheme with a silver roof. *Patrick C. Dorin and Frank Schnick*

The Rock Island business/inspection car, the Lake Michigan, is shown here in the silver color. The streamlined car was numbered 101, and was certainly a very attractive piece of equipment. The car is shown here at Chicago in June 1970. The Rock Island, by the way, was one of the few railroads that did not initially join the Amtrak system in 1971. *William Raia*

The Southern Pacific repainted their business car, SP 106, the Oregon, in the Amtrak colors. At one time in the early to mid-1970s, there was a rule that required all individual railroad cars to be painted in the Amtrak colors if they were to be part of an Amtrak train. This rule was discontinued by 1979. The SP 106 is shown here on the rear of the Coast Starlight en route from Oakland to Portland in the late 1970s. *Patrick C. Dorin*

Algoma Central's Michipicoten was built by Pullman in 1910 for the Southern Railway. The AC purchased the car in 1944. It has been used for a variety of operations including the Agawa Canyon Tour Trains. *Patrick C. Dorin*

The Great Northern painted their heavyweight business cars in the Pullman Green and Orange color scheme. The GN's A-11 is shown here as part of the consist of a Rail Fan Special. The GN numbered their business cars beginning with the letter "A." *Patrick C. Dorin*

The Green Bay and Western purchased a Union Pacific dome car and named it the Trempealeau River. It is shown here in the consist of a passenger special. When the Wisconsin Central purchased the GB&W, the car became part of the WC passenger fleet.

The new Wisconsin Central (the former Soo Line and Duluth, South Shore and Atlantic Railroad lines in Wisconsin and Michigan) purchased several cars for business car operations. The cars were painted in an attractive red and grey scheme with yellow striping. This is one of the WC's business cars in a passenger special in 1998. *Patrick C. Dorin*

The WC's Sierra Club was a rebuilt dome lounge car from the Burlington with an observation platform. Other than the Trempealeau River, very few business cars in North America were dome cars. The Sierra Club is bringing up the rear of a WC passenger special in 1998. *Patrick C. Dorin*

RAILWAYS

American Passenger Train Equipment 1940s-1980s	ISBN 1-58388-263-4
American Passenger Trains: WWII to Amtrak	ISBN 1-58388-232-4
Chicago & North Western Passenger Trains of the 400 Fleet Photo Archive	ISBN 1-58388-159-X
Chicago Stations & Trains Photo Archive	ISBN 1-58388-216-2
Chicago, St. Paul, Minneapolis & Omaha Railway 1880-1940 Photo Archive	ISBN 1-882256-67-0
Chicagoland Commuter Railroads: Metra & Northern Indiana Commuter Transportation District	ISBN 1-58388-190-5
Classic Sreamliners Photo Archive: The Trains and the Designers	ISBN 1-58388-144-x
Freight Trains of the Upper Mississippi River Photo Archive	ISBN 1-58388-136-0
Great Lakes Ore Docks and Ore Cars	ISBN 1-58388-202-2
Great Northern Railway Ore Docks of Lake Superior Photo Archive	ISBN 1-58388-073-9
Illinois Central Railroad 1854-1960 Photo Archive	ISBN 1-58388-063-1
Interurban Trains to Chicago Photo Archive	ISBN 1-58388-199-9
Locomotives of the Upper Midwest Photo Archive: Diesel Power in the 1960s and 1970s	ISBN 1-58388-113-1
Milwaukee Road 1850-1960 Photo Archive	ISBN 1-882256-61-1
Milwaukee Road Depots 1856-1954 Photo Archive	ISBN 1-58388-040-2
Northern Pacific Railway Photo Archive	ISBN 1-58388-186-7
Pacific Coast Commuter Railroads: From San Diego to Anchorage	ISBN 1-58388-221-9
Pennsylvania Railroad Locomotives: Steam, Diesel & Electric Photo Archive	ISBN 1-58388-228-6
Rio Grande Locomotives Photo Archive	ISBN 1-58388-244-8
Rock Island Railroad Photo Archive	ISBN 1-58388-265-0
Santa Fe Railway Photo Archive	ISBN 1-58388-259-6
Show Trains of the 20th Century	ISBN 1-58388-030-5
Soo Line 1975-1992 Photo Archive	ISBN 1-882256-68-9
Steam Locomotives of the B&O Railroad Photo Archive	ISBN 1-58388-095-X
Trains of the Circus 1872-1956	ISBN 1-58388-024-0
Trains of the Upper Midwest Photo Archive Steam & Diesel in the 1950s & 1960s	ISBN 1-58388-036-4
Union Pacific Railroad- Passenger Trains of the City Fleet Photo Archive	ISBN 1-58388-236-7
Washington State Railroad Depots Photo Archive	ISBN 1-58388-245-6

AUTOMOTIVE

AMC Cars 1954-1987: An Illustrated History	ISBN 1-58388-112-3
AMC Performance Cars 1951-1983 Photo Archive	ISBN 1-58388-127-1
AMX Photo Archive: From Concept to Reality	ISBN 1-58388-062-3
The American Taxi- A Century of Service	ISBN 1-58388-176-X
Avanti: The Complete Story	ISBN 1-58388-213-8
Buick 1946-1960 Photo Archive	ISBN 1-58388-178-6
Cadillac Fleetwood Seventy-Five Series Limousines Photo Archive	ISBN 1-58388-248-0
Cadillac: The Tailfin Years	ISBN 1-58388-212-X
Camaro 1967-2000 Photo Archive	ISBN 1-58388-032-1
Chevrolet Corvair Photo History	ISBN 1-58388-118-2
Chevrolet Station Wagons 1946-1966 Photo Archive	ISBN 1-58388-069-0
Classic American Limousines 1955-2000 Photo Archive	ISBN 1-58388-041-0
Cobra and Shelby Mustang Photo Archive 1962-2007 Including Prototypes and Clones	ISBN 1-58388-198-0
The Complete U.S. Automotive Sales Literature Checklist 1946-2000	ISBN 1-58388-155-7
Corvair by Chevrolet Experimental & Production Cars 1957-1969, Ludvigsen Library Series	ISBN 1-58388-058-5
Corvette The Exotic Experimental Cars, Ludvigsen Library Series	ISBN 1-58388-017-8
Corvette Prototypes & Show Cars Photo Album	ISBN 1-882256-77-8
DeTomaso Pantera	ISBN 1-58388-177-8
Encyclopedia of Small-Scale Diecast Motor Vehicle Manufacturers	ISBN 1-58388-174-3
Ferrari- The Factory Maranello's Secrets 1950-1975, Ludvigsen Library Series	ISBN 1-58388-085-2
Ford Postwar Flatheads 1946-1953 Photo Archive	ISBN 1-58388-080-1
Ford Station Wagons 1929-1991 Photo History	ISBN 1-58388-103-4
Grand Prix: Pontiac's Luxury Performance Car	ISBN 1-58388-184-0
Henney Motor Company: A Complete Story	ISBN 1-58388-233-2
Hudson Automobiles	ISBN 1-58388-266-9
Imperial 1964-1968 Photo Archive	ISBN 1-882256-23-9
It's Delightful! It's Delovely! It's DeSoto Automobiles	ISBN 1-58388-172-7
Jaguar XK120, XK140, XK150 Sports Cars Ludvigsen Library Series	ISBN 1-58388-150-6
Javelin Photo Archive: From Concept to Reality	ISBN 1-58388-071-2
Kaiser-Frazer 1947-1955 Photo Archive	ISBN 1-58388-239-1
The Lincoln Continental Story: From Zephyr to Mark II	ISBN 1-58388-154-9
Lincoln Motor Cars 1920-1942 Photo Archive	ISBN 1-882256-57-3
Mercedes-Benz 300SL: Gullwings and Roadsters 1954-1964 Ludvigsen Library Series	ISBN 1-58388-137-9
Mercury Automobiles 1939-1959	ISBN 1-58388-205-7
Miller-Meteor: The Complete Illustrated History	ISBN 1-58388-258-8
MG Saloons and Coupes 1925-1980	ISBN 1-58388-144-1
Nash 1936-1957 Photo Archive	ISBN 1-58388-086-0
Oldsmobile 1946-1960 Photo Archive	ISBN 1-58388-168-9
Packard Motor Cars 1946-1958 Photo Archive	ISBN 1-882256-45-X
Pontiac Dream Cars, Show Cars & Prototypes 1928-1998 Photo Album	ISBN 1-882256-93-X
Pontiac's Greatest Decade 1959-1969—The Wide Track Era: An Illustrated History	ISBN 1-58388-163-8
Rambler 1950-1969 Photo Archive	ISBN 1-58388-078-X
Stretch Limousines 1928-2001 Photo Archive	ISBN 1-58388-070-4
Studebaker Lark 1959-1966 Photo Archive	ISBN 1-58388-107-7
The Collector's Guide to GTO 1964-1974	ISBN 1-58388-196-4
Thirty Years of the Volkswagen Golf & Rabbit	ISBN 1-58388-158-1
Ultimate Corvette Trivia Challenge	ISBN 1-58388-035-6

BUSES

Buses of ACF Photo Archive Including ACF-Brill And CCF-Brill	ISBN 1-58388-101-8
Buses of Motor Coach Industries 1932-2000 Photo Archive	ISBN 1-58388-039-9
Buses of Western Flyer and New Flyer Industries Photo Archive	ISBN 1-58388-229-4
City Transit Buses of the 20th Century Photo Gallery	ISBN 1-58388-146-8
Fageol & Twin Coach Buses 1922-1956 Photo Archive	ISBN 1-58388-075-5
Flxible Intercity Buses 1924-1970 Photo Archive	ISBN 1-58388-108-5
Flxible Transit Buses 1953-1995 Photo Archive	ISBN 1-58388-053-4
GM Intercity Coaches 1944-1980 Photo Archive	ISBN 1-58388-099-2
Going the Greyhound Way: The Romance of the Road	ISBN 1-58388-246-4
Greyhound in Postcards: Buses, Depots and Posthouses	ISBN 1-58388-130-1
Highway Buses of the 20th Century Photo Gallery	ISBN 1-58388-121-2
Mack® Buses 1900-1960 Photo Archive*	ISBN 1-58388-020-8
Museum of Bus Transportation Presents: Motorcoach Milestones	ISBN 1-58388-260-X
New York City Transit Buses 1945-1975 Photo Archive	ISBN 1-58388-149-2
New York Fifth Avenue Coach Co. 1885-1960	ISBN 1-58388-249-9
Old Look Buses: Yellow Coach and GM in the 40s and 50s	ISBN 1-58388-256-1
Prevost Buses 1924-2002 Photo Archive	ISBN 1-58388-083-6
Rapid Transit Series Buses: General Motors and Beyond	ISBN 1-58388-209-X
Trailways Buses 1936-2001 Photo Archive	ISBN 1-58388-029-1
Trolley Buses 1913-2001 Photo Archive	ISBN 1-58388-057-7
Trolley Buses Around the World: A Photo Gallery	ISBN 1-58388-175-1
Welcome Aboard the GM New Look Bus: An Enthusiast's Reference	ISBN 1-58388-167-5
Yellow Coach Buses 1923-1943 Photo Archive	ISBN 1-58388-054-2

TRUCKS

4x4 Offroad Racing Trucks	ISBN 1-58388-243-X
AM General: Hummers, Mutts, Buses & Postal Jeeps	ISBN 1-58388-135-2
Autocar Trucks of the 1950s At Work	ISBN 1-58388-231-6
Autocar Trucks of the 1960s At Work	ISBN 1-58388-241-3
Autocar Trucks 1899-1950 Photo Archive	ISBN 1-58388-115-8
Brockway Trucks 1948-1961 Photo Archive*	ISBN 1-882256-55-7
Chevrolet El Camino Photo History Incl. GMC Sprint & Caballero	ISBN 1-58388-044-5
Circus and Carnival Trucks 1923-2000 Photo Archive	ISBN 1-58388-048-8
Diamond T Trucks 1911-1966 Photo Archive	ISBN 1-58388-204-9
Dodge C-Series Trucks Restorer's & Collector's Reference Guide and History	ISBN 1-58388-140-9
Dodge Heavy-Duty Trucks 1928-1975	ISBN 1-58388-194-8
Dodge Pickups 1939-1978 Photo Album	ISBN 1-882256-82-4
Dodge Ram Trucks 1994-2001 Photo History	ISBN 1-58388-051-8
Dodge Trucks 1948-1960 Photo Archive	ISBN 1-882256-37-9
El Camino by Chevrolet	ISBN 1-58388-215-4
Federal Trucks Photo Archive	ISBN 1-58388-223-5
Ford Medium-Duty Trucks 1917-1998 Photo History	ISBN 1-58388-162-X
Ford Ranchero 1957-1979 Photo History	ISBN 1-58388-126-3
Freightliner Trucks 1937-1981 Photo Archive	ISBN 1-58388-090-9
FWD Trucks 1910-1974 Photo Archive	ISBN 1-58388-142-5
GMC Light-Duty Trucks	ISBN 1-58388-191-3
International Heavy Trucks of the 1950s: At Work	ISBN 1-58388-160-3
International Heavy Trucks of the 1960s: At Work	ISBN 1-58388-161-1
Jeep 1941-2000 Photo Archive	ISBN 1-58388-021-6
Jeep Prototypes & Concept Vehicles Photo Archive	ISBN 1-58388-033-X
Kenworth Trucks 1950-1979 At Work	ISBN 1-58388-147-6
Land Rover: The Incomparable 4x4 from Series 1 to Defender, Ludvigsen Library Series	ISBN 1-58388-179-4
Mack Model AB Photo Archive*	ISBN 1-882256-18-2
Mack AP Super-Duty Trucks 1926-1938 Photo Archive*	ISBN 1-882256-54-9
Mack Model B 1953-1966 Volume 2 Photo Archive*	ISBN 1-882256-34-4
Mack EB-EC-ED-EE-EF-EG-DE 1936-1951 Photo Archive*	ISBN 1-882256-29-8
Mack FC-FCSW-NW 1936-1947 Photo Archive*	ISBN 1-882256-28-X
Mack LF-LH-LJ-LM-LT 1940-1956 Photo Archive*	ISBN 1-882256-38-7
Muscle Trucks: High-Performance Pickups	ISBN 1-58388-197-2
Peterbilt Trucks 1939-1979 At Work	ISBN 1-58388-152-2
Refuse Trucks Photo Archive	ISBN 1-58388-042-9
Reo Trucks 1910-1966 Photo Archive	ISBN 1-58388-181-6
Semi Trucks of the 1950s: A Photo Gallery	ISBN 1-58388-187-5
Studebaker Trucks 1927-1940 Photo Archive	ISBN 1-882256-40-9
The Long Haul: American Trucking Companies	ISBN 1-58388-211-1
White-Freightliner Trucks of the 1960s At Work	ISBN 1-58388-264-2
White Trucks of the 1950s At Work	ISBN 1-58388-230-8
White Trucks of the 1960s At Work	ISBN 1-58388-240-5
White Trucks 1900-1937 Photo Archive	ISBN 1-882256-80-8

More Great Titles From Iconografix

All Iconografix books are available from direct mail specialty book dealers and bookstores worldwide, or can be ordered from the publisher. For book trade and distribution information or to add your name to our mailing list and receive a **FREE CATALOG** contact:

Iconografix, Inc.
PO Box 446, Dept BK, Hudson, WI, 54016
Telephone: (715) 381-9755, (800) 289-3504 (USA), Fax: (715) 381-9756
info@iconografixinc.com
www.iconografixinc.com

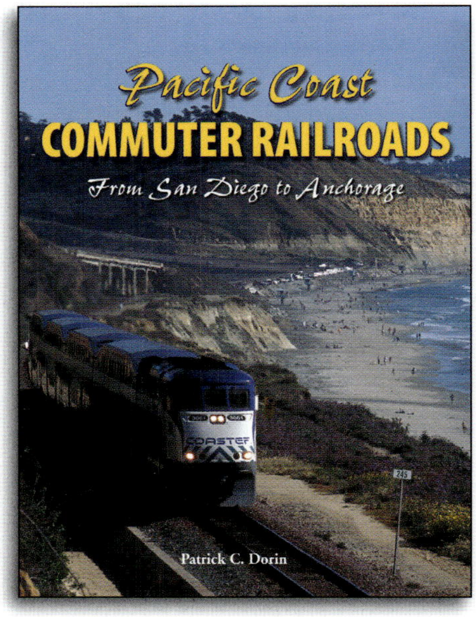

ISBN 978-1-58388-221-4

ISBN 978-1-58388-232-0

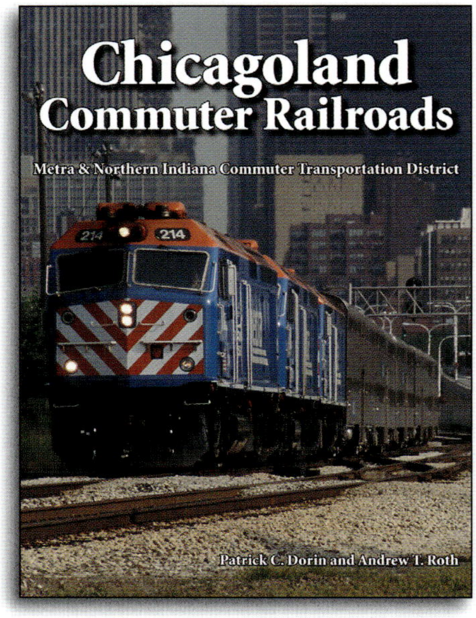

ISBN 978-1-58388-190-3

More great books from Iconografix

ISBN 978-1-58388-216-0

Iconografix, Inc.
P.O. Box 446, Dept BK,
Hudson, WI 54016
For a free catalog call:
1-800-289-3504
info@iconografixinc.com
www.iconografixinc.com

ISBN 978-1-58388-245-0

ISBN 978-1-58388-259-7

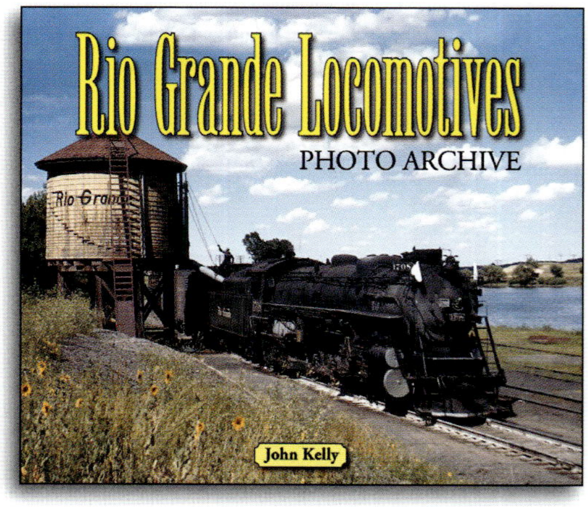

ISBN 978-1-58388-244-3